Extraordinary
INFLUENCE

Extraordinary
INFLUENCE

How
Great Leaders
Bring Out the Best
in Others

Tim Irwin, Ph.D.

WILEY

Published by John Wiley & Sons, Inc., Hoboken, New Jersey.
Published simultaneously in Canada.

For general information on our other products and services or for technical support, please contact our Customer Care Department within the United States at (800) 762-2974, outside the United States at (317) 572-3993 or fax (317) 572-4002.

Wiley publishes in a variety of print and electronic formats and by print-on-demand. Some material included with standard print versions of this book may not be included in e-books or in print-on-demand. If this book refers to media such as a CD or DVD that is not included in the version you purchased, you may download this material at http://booksupport.wiley.com. For more information about Wiley products, visit www.wiley.com.

Library of Congress Cataloging-in-Publication Data:

Names: Irwin, Tim, 1949–
Title: Extraordinary influence : how great leaders bring out the best in
 others / Tim Irwin.
Description: Hoboken : Wiley, 2018. | Includes index. |
Identifiers: LCCN 2017058808 (print) | LCCN 2018000083 (ebook) | ISBN
 9781119464440 (pdf) | ISBN 9781119464433 (epub) | ISBN 9781119464426
 (hardback) | ISBN 9781119464440 (ePDF)
Subjects: LCSH: Leadership. | Personnel management. | BISAC: BUSINESS &
 ECONOMICS / Human Resources & Personnel Management. | BUSINESS &
 ECONOMICS / Leadership. | BUSINESS & ECONOMICS / Management.
Classification: LCC HD57.7 (ebook) | LCC HD57.7 .I793 2018 (print) | DDC
 658.4/092—dc23
LC record available at https://lccn.loc.gov/2017058808

Cover Design: Wiley

Printed in the United States of America

10 9 8 7 6 5 4 3 2 1

To my Clients, from whom I have learned so much over the years.

CONTENTS

FOREWORD

Tim Tassopoulos
President and Chief Operating Office, Chick-fil-A

I am grateful that one of the mentors who has wielded "extraordinary influence" in my life is Dr. Tim Irwin. Tim is a consultant to many of America's most respected organizations and Fortune 100 companies. His faith is evident, his love for family and friends is unshakeable, and his commitment to developing others is impressive. That's the heart behind this book.

My relationship with Tim started over 30 years ago. Tim was an advisor and consultant to Chick-fil-A founder, Truett Cathy, and Chick-fil-A president, Jimmy Collins. As the generations of Chick-fil-A leadership changed over time, Tim's insights, counsel, and active consulting about talent management, organizational effectiveness, leadership development, and culture have made a tremendous contribution to our company and its leaders. I encourage you to read this book to glean your own insights as a leader, teacher, coach, or parent, from Tim's broad and practical book.

Smart people have different definitions of leadership. Warren Bennis defined leadership as the capacity to "translate intention into reality and sustain it." Marcus Buckingham, author and consultant, says that leaders "rally people to a better future." John Maxwell, pastor and author, says, "Leadership is influence—nothing more, nothing less." I find value in each of these perspectives, but Tim Irwin's definition of leadership as "extraordinary influence" aligns with my own personal definition. *Extraordinary influence* is ultimately how one person positively impacts others through choice and not through forced compliance. This is real leadership—not the power or prestige that is often confused with strong leadership.

What is the one, essential quality of a leader who wants to make an impact in a positive way? What matters most for the leader who wants to leave a meaningful legacy for the next generation? What capacity should a leader develop most to fuel their leadership engine? The answer to each of these questions is the same—extraordinary influence.

I encourage you to read, reflect, and apply—put the leadership principles found in this book into practice, as I have. Become an inspiring leader known for extraordinary influence. Develop your character as a leader. Then, dare to lead!

Part I
The Science
of Extraordinary
Influence

1 The Blue Suitcase Phenomenon

Many Leaders Create an Effect They Did Not Intend

A few years ago, a group invited me to speak to their annual leadership conference in Europe, and they included my family on the trip. A month or so before our departure, my wife, Anne, told me about a lifelong dream to visit Portugal and wondered if we could stop in Lisbon on the way to the meeting. Our travel agent told her that our airfare would change only slightly, so I said somewhat distractedly, "Fine with me." Anne made the hotel arrangements, and I moved the departure date up on my calendar.

Just days before we left for our trip, the hotel confirmation arrived. I went into shock when I saw the exorbitant charge for our hotel stay in Portugal and asked Anne with visible irritation, "How can we afford this? There is no way we have enough money to stay in that hotel." Anne calmly explained that she was upset, too, but it was the only hotel that had space available. She then shared her plan to save money by bringing our food with us. Anne brought down the old blue suitcase from the attic and filled it with food for our four days in Portugal. At that point, it was too late to change our flights without a significant penalty, so we moved ahead with her plan.

After flying all night, Anne, our two sons, and I checked into the beautiful Hotel Estoril del Sol, a magnificent beachfront property in Lisbon and ate our first breakfast from the food Anne packed in the blue suitcase. I opened a miniature box of cereal with my Swiss Army knife and squirted it with room temperature milk from a small carton that needed no refrigeration. My father always described his two grandsons as "appetites with skin stretched over them," and you could tell from the faces of our two sons that the Blue Suitcase Plan was not getting off to a good start! The view of the Atlantic Ocean was beautiful, but the breakfast was dreadful. Anne noted our grumpy moods and suggested we change clothes and begin our tour of Lisbon.

On the way down, our elevator stopped on the mezzanine level. As the doors parted, we looked straight into the hotel dining room. It looked like a spectacular movie set. With a backdrop of the bluest ocean I'd ever seen, linen-draped tables were laden with magnificent food. Large ice swans and flowers decorated the tables as pleasant servers attentively bustled around. What I noticed most, however, was how happy everyone in the dining room seemed to be. I knew the reason they were happy—they were eating breakfast in that beautiful dining room!

Sensing trouble, Anne pulled my arm and led us down the stairs out into the bright Portuguese sunshine. After several hours of sightseeing, we stopped for lunch in a park with a shady bench overlooking the magnificent bay. Anne handed me a can of tuna fish with a pull top ring and some saltines—our lunch. I felt grateful for her resourcefulness, but these types of meals went on for four days. Our boys bordered on hostility and aggression after being denied their normal caloric intake for that long. They were in that preadolescent growth phase when they ate constantly and only became taller.

The night before our departure, I stopped to check our bill with the front desk clerk. As I turned to leave, she said pleasantly, "Mr. Irwin, may I make your breakfast reservation in the hotel dining room tomorrow morning before you leave for the airport?" Not understanding the comment, I turned and asked her to explain. "Of course, *all of your meals are included in the room fee.*" In a millisecond, it all became clear! The reason the hotel was so expensive was that our meals were included in the price of the room. We had just spent four days eating the most awful food I could remember, when we could have been eating in the beautiful hotel dining room with all the other happy guests. The bitter irony was that we had to leave for the airport the next morning before the restaurant opened, so we even missed the one meal that we still had coming!

In defense of my incredibly smart wife, Anne had asked about meals when she made the reservation. Something obviously was lost in the translation between the hotel and our travel agent.

Where Does Your Organization Eat?

It is always surprising to me how so many organizations eat out of the blue suitcase of mediocre performance when both the leaders and the workers themselves long to eat in the beautiful dining room of exceptional performance. What's the difference between those organizations that eat out of the suitcase versus in the dining room? While economic conditions and strategic decisions on how best to capitalize on market opportunities make a huge difference, ultimately, the performance of the people in the organization determine its fate.

We see some organizations with happy, motivated employees solving problems, delighting customers, and working hard to reach goals. We observe others with a dreadful culture of rude employees who transfer us to the wrong department, or when we call their 800 number for customer support, the person on the phone acts as if we were a complete idiot. When I call in for computer support, that depiction may be justified—I just don't want to be treated that way.

Engagement surveys should dishearten any of us who want our organizations to prosper. Gallup reported that 67% of workers are disengaged in the workplace. Even more disconcerting is that in the disengaged group, 17.2% are "actively disengaged,"[1] meaning that they seek to work as little as possible.

We've watched *Office Space* and laughed at the scene where Bob, the consultant, interviews Peter, one of the workers at Initech.

BOB SLYDELL: Y'see, what we're trying to do here, we're just trying to get a feel for how people spend their day. So, if you would, would you just walk us through a typical day for you?

PETER: Yeah.

BOB SLYDELL: Great.

PETER: Well, I generally come in at least 15 minutes late. I use the sidedoor, that way Lumbergh can't see me. Uh, and after that, I just sorta space out for about an hour.

BOB PORTER: Space out?

PETER: Yeah. I just stare at my desk but it looks like I'm working. I do that for probably another hour after lunch, too. I'd probably, say, in a given week, I probably do about 15 minutes of real, actual work.[2]

We laugh but also quietly wonder if Peter works for us. While *Office Space* seems farcical on its face, it also touches a nerve. The Gallup and other data suggest there are more Peters in the workplace than we might assume.

Many view their jobs as a penalty box between weekends. They find little to no hope that their work will ever provide more than a paycheck to pay some bills and to enable the pursuit of fulfillment elsewhere.

I frequently speak to groups of senior executives and often ask a question. "How many of you feel that maybe not all, but many of the employees working in your organization are capable of making a higher contribution to the organization than they currently are?" It's rare when I do not get close to a 100% "yes" to that question. I then ask a more difficult but related question. "If they can make a higher contribution to your organization, then why aren't they?" What corporate leader, what parent, what coach doesn't want to release the extraordinary potential of the employees, players, students, or children under their influence? Isn't it a critical part of our job to figure this out?

The reality is that this challenge extends far beyond the corporate environment. What parent hasn't agonized over how to get a seemingly unmotivated child to care about school and their future? What teacher hasn't begun his or her career with the idealistic aspiration of stoking the flames of intrinsic motivation and transforming their lackluster students into talented academic performers? What coach hasn't longed to find the key to unlock a gifted but underperforming athlete's potential? Scout leaders, religious, and other community leaders and anyone who seeks to make a difference in others' lives wrestles with the question, "How do I get another person to rise above the daily-ness of their lives to perform beyond what anyone thought possible?"

The age-old question for every organization—how do we bring out the best in those we are responsible for leading? How do we get them to care? How do we ensure productivity, quality, timeliness, and great attention to customers? How do we help them love their jobs? These represent the most pivotal questions that should keep any competent, conscientious leader awake at night. What makes this especially vexing rests in the reality that the answer to the above questions seems to vary widely among different employees.

Do we know anyone who says I want to go work today and see how badly I can screw up? Do we know anyone who says I really want to work for a firm which embarrasses me when I tell others where I work? My sense is that employees long to eat in the dining room of excellence as much as their leaders. Most want to be proud of their work and the reputation of the organizations they serve. Despite the inherently positive predisposition of many workers, think about how many organizations languish with terrible customer service, high turnover, and marginal engagement in the work.

The Conundrum

Like most young families, my wife, Anne, and I looked for age-appropriate chores that could be assigned to our two sons for teaching responsibility and self-discipline. Anne took the lead on asking our sons to take out the kitchen garbage every day. There is very little difference between getting children to take out the garbage and running a Fortune 500 company—well, maybe scale and complexity, but some of the fundamentals are the same. How do you motivate another person to do something with quality, speed, and consistency? For some odd reason, the fact that the boys' allowance (their weekly salary) was predicated on getting the garbage out and doing some other chores didn't seem to make that much difference. Neither did the fact that Anne was the parent. As I tell CEOs quite often, position power is not all it's cracked up to be. Anne often resorted to nagging, occasional yelling or fearsome threats, like no TV for a week, which produced short-term results but certainly nothing sustainable. None of these management techniques accomplished anything that transformed our two young sons into conscientious, happy, quality-insuring garbage taker-outers.

How we motivate another person or group of people to do something and do it well is a conundrum. Anyone who has raised a family, led an army, run a company, or coached a team struggles to find the key to motivate an individual person to excel, to realize his or her potential, and to get an important job done well. It is surprising how often we resort to a default position of a negative consequence for not doing something versus an approach that actually results in a better worker and a better person.

Ultimately, don't we hope to foster intrinsic motivation so that the individuals we lead become better employees, better students, or better athletes, and so on. Anne wanted the garbage taken out for sure, but what she and I really wanted was for our gangly teenagers to mature and to eventually have responsible jobs and healthy, accomplished families of their own. She and I longed for our sons to pursue some high and noble purpose with their lives and to make a difference in the world. Maybe running a Fortune 500 company is easier after all!

Task-Driven Leadership

Let me speak to skeptics. Over the years, I've interviewed thousands of leaders, many of whom were hard-driving and task-focused. While giving intellectual assent to the relational aspect of work, these leaders often disparage the soft skills of management. Even as an organizational psychologist, supposedly an expert on the soft side of management, I admit that some of the stuff I read is way too spineless for me, as well. For those readers who are skeptics, try to remain open as I attempt to make a case for the major thesis of this book—we gain an extraordinary ability to transform others when we affirm them versus when we apply what might euphemistically be called *constructive criticism*. Hopefully, you might adopt recommendations from this book strictly out of pragmatism, if nothing else.

Many of the things we do to motivate others, in fact, accomplish the exact opposite of what we intend.

I have consulted with hundreds of organizations during my career. I've heard many task-driven leaders espouse their philosophy of leadership, often in short pithy phrases. Several weeks ago, I sat with a senior leader, who said with great fanfare and sincerity, "I believe people don't do what you expect, they do what you inspect." She smiled at me looking for affirmation that she had finally unlocked the secret to motivation. I didn't want to deflate her and explain how many times I'd heard that hackneyed phrase over the years. Certainly, it is true that inexperienced workers need more direction, structure, and feedback, but this involves a lot more than inspection.

Here are some other phrases we hear routinely from the task-driven style of leadership.

"I'm going to hold his feet to the fire."—Origin: a method of torture to force heretics to recant in the Middle Ages.

"I need to light a fire under her."—A phrase originally used to motivate chimney sweeps who feared climbing to the top inside a high chimney.

"I'm going to hold you accountable."—*Accountable* is derived from the Old French word *acont*, such as counting money. The connotation is the thinly veiled threat that you better do what I said to do. We are reminded of the not-so-jolly aspect of Santa's personality—"keeping a list and checking it twice."

"One throat to choke."—On a given initiative, the idea is that you need one person who is accountable for the results.

"There's nothing so clarifying as a good public hanging."—When someone does not perform according to expectations, his firing can be used as an example for what happens to those who don't achieve targeted results.

"He needs some fire in the belly."—The source of the expression is not known, but it's conjectured that this metaphor for motivation comes from stoking a potbellied stove.

"I got in his face."—A direct and aggressive management style intended to provoke action.

"Next time I'm going to write you up."—A common practice in some organizations thought to intimidate workers to comply under the inherent threat, "You do this again and you're fired."

"I'm going to work you so hard, your [private parts] will sweat."— I overheard this profane expression used ostensibly to motivate a mid-level manager in a Fortune 500 company, which prided itself on forward-thinking human resource practices.

Macho Management

We have all heard many of these commonly used phrases and maybe even said them ourselves. I like to think of this approach to motivation of employees as *Macho Management*. "I'm tough-minded and in control. I will get you to do what I want done." If we take out the often good intentions behind the statements, aren't they a bit self-righteous? Aren't they a bit patronizing? Aren't they assuming the worst about human nature?

Do most leaders brazenly act this way? No, it's typically a more subtle management style. The inherent belief reflected in these sayings is that *I'm going to get you to do something you are fundamentally resistant to doing*. If we look under the hood of Macho Management, it suggests that workers or students or players or children are lazy, irresponsible, lacking ambition, and less intelligent, and therefore require constant scrutiny to ensure that work gets done. We might say, "That's a bit harsh." True, but in our drive to get results out of the people we manage or teach or coach or parent, we may adopt methods that appeal to our fundamental need to control outcomes. A question that should keep us up at night is whether there is a way to transform those we lead so that they are internally motivated to achieve excellence without all that brash fanfare. No one who's been a leader believes it's easy to get someone to change. No one who has parented, taught, coached, or led people into battle thinks those jobs are easy, either.

Common practices in management today are strikingly different from what new science teaches us and should not be ignored even by those with a track record of success.

If you are a corporate leader, you likely reached your lofty perch by performing your job well and getting others to perform theirs. Many task-driven leaders excel at getting things done. Their demanding expectations achieve results; however, it's now clear from a growing body of research that for a leader to be effective, it's vital that we spend time and energy in both task-oriented management as well as a framework that values the *emotional and relational dimensions of the people we lead*. Addressing our employees' emotional side has a neurobiological basis that heavily influences the performance of workers. This neurological evidence, which will be presented in subsequent chapters, will likely surprise you and may provide compelling conviction even for task-oriented leaders that there's something of substance to the emotional side of a worker's motivation. Common practices in management today are strikingly different from what science teaches us and should not be ignored even by those with a track record of success.

Bring Out the Best in Others

So, how do we bring out the best in others? What is the secret to helping another person unlock his or her potential? If we knew how to bring out the best characteristics in those we lead, wouldn't we do it? Most leaders hope to exert significant, maybe even extraordinary influence on those they lead and to bring out the best in them. They likely want their followers to flourish personally and, understandably, to perform their jobs to the benefit of the organization they serve. This yearning for the success of others is no different for parents, teachers, coaches, military leaders, and anyone who leads.

Here's the challenge. Recent brain research argues that *many of the things we do to motivate others, in fact, accomplishes the exact opposite of what we intend.* We inadvertently engage the wrong part of the brain, thus short-circuiting what influence we might want to have, such as advancing that person along a meaningful developmental trajectory.

They worked at it with all their heart.

One of my favorite stories from ancient literature is about a man who was charged with rebuilding a vitally important wall to protect a city using a volunteer labor force, whose only building material was damaged rubble from the former wall. During the process of accomplishing what many critics described as impossible, one observer said of the people building the wall, "They worked at it with all their heart."[3]

What if we could get people to work with all their heart? What if we could transform those under our influence in such a way that the fires of intrinsic motivation burned brightly and those people found great purpose in their work? Isn't that what we want as leaders, parents, or teachers? We want to transform the attitudes, the work habits, and the passion of those we influence—to get them to do the assigned task, even take out the garbage, with a sense of commitment and energy.

Recent discoveries of brain science coupled with the wisdom of top CEOs, whom I interviewed for this book, give us the answers we've long sought. Chapter 2 opens with a story about a young man who was deeply impacted by some words aptly spoken.

Notes

1. http://www.gallup.com/poll/188144/employee-engagement-stagnant-2015.aspx.
2. http://www.imsdb.com/scripts/Office-Space.html.
3. Nehemiah 4:6 (New International Version).

2 Words of Life

New Brain Research Explains How We Bring Out the Best in Others

William was inconsolable. His sweat-drenched hair against my face, I held my son as his body shook with heaving sobs. The game, the season, the countless predawn weight room sessions, and two-a-day practices—the investment of eight years of his young life all came down to one Friday night. As co-captain, he had devoted everything to inspire this team of young men to surpass everyone's expectations.

Earlier that evening, an electric atmosphere warmed the chilly December night. It was true Norman Rockwell Americana—lush green turf with perfect white stripes brilliantly illuminated, animated cheerleaders at their practiced best, bands blaring, and the intense pregame warm-ups anticipating the epic battle about to unfold.

This was no ordinary game. It was the second round of the high school state football playoffs. The teams' energy quickly transformed the waiting crowds into a fever-pitched frenzy—both sides desperately wanting their team to prevail. I was the proudest dad on the planet as I watched my son walk out to midfield for the coin toss.

An epic battle it was. Neither team lost that night, even though the opposing team had more points on the scoreboard and advanced to the semifinals. Behind by two touchdowns at the half, our team fought back fiercely, almost tying the game in the closing minutes.

When the final seconds ticked off the scoreboard clock, the families walked on to the field to meet their sons. I held my heartbroken son, and the tears streaming down his swollen, bruised face captured what we all felt—the bitter disappointment of losing and the sadness felt by 12 seniors and their families. This would be the last of their "Friday night lights."

As steam from William's overheated body rose into the cold night air, I noticed the head coach of the opposing team walking across the field directly toward us. He came close and said, "Sir, may I speak with your son?"

I moved away as he put his hands on my son's shoulders and looked directly into his reddened eyes. Barely audible to me, I heard the coach say some surprising words to this young player from the opposing team. "Son, tonight you played an outstanding game, and you left nothing on the field. You displayed great character and courage in the way that you led your teammates, and it was an honor to play against you." He smiled, hugged William, and then walked the length of the field to the end zone, where his celebrating team drowned out the other sounds of the night.

Not long after, I learned that the coach who spoke with my son that night was known for the impact he had on countless football players—many of his own and sometimes players from other teams as in the case of my son.

Over time, I came to understand how deeply those words had lodged in William's core. How did this coach exert such extraordinary influence? He spoke *Words of Life* transformed him. Six months later, William entered the crucible of Plebe Summer at the United States Naval Academy in Annapolis, Maryland. The next four years he faced a grueling regimen of academic, physical, and emotional challenges. He experienced college football career-ending injuries, including a broken back. After graduation from the academy he began another gauntlet, which included nuclear engineering school, the submarine warfare program, and the U.S. Navy diving school. After seven-and-a half years of highly stressful covert deployments, he left the Navy to attend business school for two years and then entered the business world.

One particular coach's Words of Life and many other key influencers in my son's life created beliefs that took root in his core and still direct his actions today. Affirmations across the span of his life fostered beliefs that became firmly ensconced in his inner person, such as, "While what I'm going through is incredibly difficult, I can finish this. There is great value in excellence, and I must model this for those I lead. I will endure the hardship and be stronger and better equipped to lead others regardless of the difficulties we face."

Isn't this what we want—someone who will speak Words of Life to us? "You displayed great courage and integrity. You accomplished far more than you even thought possible." Anyone with a leadership role, whether a manager in a corporate setting, a parent, a teacher, a coach, a scout master, or a religious leader, possesses the potential to exert extraordinary influence in others' lives. They can literally bring out the best in us.

Pulled by Purpose

Why do we want affirmation? Of course, it feels good, but why? Aristotle observed that every person is drawn by a *telos* or purpose in their lives. I believe that, deep down, we want to know that we gave it our all to pursue high and noble ends and to realize a deep sense of significance in our lives. We long for confirmation that, in fact, our lives count for something more than just fighting grid-locked traffic. While our ancestors focused more on maintaining security day-to-day, this basic need is not so primary for most of us. Significance takes priority as the main driver of what we seek in life. The right kind of affirmation satisfies this compelling need. Deep affirmation gets to our core and affirms who we aspire to be.

What do we really want? Certainly, we want security—a roof over our heads, warmth in the winter and cool in the summer, food for the week, transportation, and safety, which may be higher on the list in the last few years. Once those are basically satisfied, we want significance. We want to know that our lives count for something meaningful. We sometimes get that at work, although most do not. Sometimes we must look outside work in our faith, our community, services for the aging, care for the environment, and a host of other options, but we want a sense of purpose—that we're doing something meaningful.

The most powerful personal affirmation occurs when another person acknowledges the strength of our character.

Although it is very satisfying to know deep down that we are pursuing purpose, perhaps the most powerful personal affirmation occurs when another person acknowledges the strength of our character. When someone of significance affirms us particularly in a deep way, certain beliefs are formed. These beliefs are stored in our core—that person living inside us who thinks, feels, forms opinions, and quietly speaks to us. As opportunities and circumstances occur, beliefs direct our actions. Research has shown that affirmation from others whom we respect forms beliefs in our core that guide our actions.

Our Brains Love Affirmation

In recent years, science has revealed that affirmation sets in motion huge positive changes in the brain. It releases certain neurochemicals associated with well-being and higher performance. Amazingly, criticism creates just the opposite neural reaction. The most primitive part of the brain goes into hyper defense mode, compromising our performance, torpedoing our motivation, and limiting access to our higher-order strengths. Criticism feeds a *negativity bias*, which exists in all of us. The brain constantly scans the environment for threats and diminishes our positive and creative resources.

> *In recent years, science has revealed that affirmation sets in motion huge positive changes in the brain.*

As we explored in Chapter 1, seasoned, crusty leaders dismiss what they call the *soft skills*. This subtle disparagement is juxtaposed against the *hard skills*—those required to make or sell the product. We now know that there is nothing soft about affirmation. The hard facts of science demonstrate that if you want to bring out the best in others, you must affirm them in prescribed ways. If you want to diminish their creativity and resourcefulness, then use harsh criticism.

Sometimes we are fortunate to have a person in our lives who awakens that longing for purpose and significance and affirms that we can achieve remarkable accomplishments or display great courage in the face of adversity. Some organizations also foster a culture that is encouraging and positive.

I will never forget Mrs. Wells, my high school English teacher, and Mrs. Chapman, my high school math teacher, who both awakened a desire in me to excel. They both recognized that I could do far better than the academic mediocrity, which had so thoroughly characterized my life to that point. They both saw my potential and found a way to transform my own expectations. Mr. Randolph, my boss in the shoe store where I had my first real job at 15, affirmed my ability to work with people and to influence them. These three individuals believed in me, affirmed me, and changed my beliefs about what I could accomplish with my life. Of course, they corrected my mistakes, but it was against a backdrop of affirmation and positive expectations and in a context of what I had done well.

Other experiences in life drain us of courage and extinguish
any ember of intrinsic motivation. A boss whose face seemed to be
permanently frozen in the expression of disapproval chides us and
withers our motivation with her blistering critique. The coach who
yelled at us to change what we were doing with little to no expla-
nation of how to run the play differently recycles over and over in
our memory. One of the terrible consequences I see in the corporate
world, where I spend the most of my time, is a persistently cynical
and negative culture that disheartens and saps the spirit of even the
most resilient people. A learned helplessness prevails in that company's
workforce.

I believe we can influence our employees, our organizations, our
families, our teams, and other groups for the good through affirmation.
Any type of affirmation has value but some types offer life-changing
value. We will explore the different types in Chapters 3 and 4.

Not Really Affirmation

Not long ago, Anne and I went to an engagement party for a neigh-
bor's daughter and her fiancé. The hosts' home was beautiful, and
they had recently built a large gazeebo, perfect for a genteel, southern
garden party. The grass was flawlessly manicured and the stunning
rose garden alongside the gazeebo looked like a photo shoot from
Architectural Digest. My wife, Anne, looked rather fetching that night,
as well!

At parties, Anne and I usually end up drifting apart to talk with
different people. Although I was visiting with some friends across the
room, I overheard a woman walk up to Anne and say, "Oh Anne, your
shoes are sooooo cute!" Each monosyllabic word in the previous sentence was stretched into at least three syllables for emphasis! The level
of energy and intensity in her voice might have been better suited for a
tornado warning in the neighborhood.

Now, being an old shoe dog myself (I sold shoes in high school and college), I know something about foot fashion. Anne's shoes were very attractive and really complimented her dress, but did they rise to the level of hyperbole that her friend offered up? Probably not. It might have been the wine talking but more likely it was simply her being friendly and enthusiastic. She was complimenting Anne as a social gesture to enter the conversation. It was a fun occasion, and most of the guests were being gracious and affirming. No surprise, but in none of my conversations that evening did anyone ask me if I was actively making progress in accomplishing my life purpose. That is *not* typical party banter.

There is a huge difference between affirmation and a pat on the back.

A compliment goes skin deep. It conveys esteem and appreciation but not a deep affirmation of who we are. Compliments are by their very nature superficial social rituals. They are perfect for the social customs we need in our lives to be polite and civil. Did the encounter about Anne's shoes change her life? Not in the slightest. Her friend's compliment flattered her; however, nothing of substance was transacted.

The CEOs who I interviewed for this book made it clear that there is a huge difference between affirmation and a pat on the back. Compliments provide a certain happy lift to others, but affirmation, especially when it meets certain conditions, profoundly changes us! The word affirmation originates from the Latin *affirmationem,* which means to make steady, to confirm, and *to strengthen.*[1] The deepest form of affirmation strengthens our core—our very sense of self.

Our brains benefit dramatically from affirmation. They *light up* with electrical activity. We feel more optimistic and work more productively. Conversely, criticism activates different parts of the brain that metaphorically makes us *go dark.*

Brain research indicates that affirmation:[2]

1. Buffers stress[3] and improves higher cognitive thinking[4] and problem-solving.[5]

2. Positively affects a region of the brain associated with subjective value,[6] that is, the location of *self-worth*.[7] The ventromedial prefrontal cortex evaluates how we subjectively feel about ourselves. Affirmation raises the index of our self-worth.

3. Improves self-control and makes us more efficient.[8]

4. Makes us happier and more productive.[9]

5. Activates the ventromedial prefrontal cortex, which is related to positive behavior changes.[10,11]

6. Activates brain circuits that are affected by the release of hormones like oxytocin and vasopressin, both known for their role in trust and attachment.[12]

7. Activates the parasympathetic nervous system responses,[13] which support immune health, cardiovascular health, and hormone balance.

8. Fosters innovation—it activates areas of the brain associated with calmness and openness to new ideas.[14]

Affirmation changes us for the better and can even alter our appearance. I greatly enjoyed the documentary *Jiro Dreams of Sushi*.[15] Jiro Ono owns and operates a sushi restaurant in Ginza, Chūō, Tokyo, Japan, called Sukiyabashi Jiro. The Michelin Guide awarded 3 stars to this world-renowned sushi restaurant—clearly the best in the world.

Jiro exemplifies the stern, demanding, and high-expectation leader. An apprentice chef, Daisuke Nakazawa, labors for 10 years hoping to receive Jiro's ultimate affirmation. In the documentary, Nakazawa says,

After about 10 years, they let you cook the eggs. I had been practicing making the egg sushi for a long time. I thought I would be good at it. But when it came to making the real thing ... I kept messing up. I was making up to four a day. But they kept saying, "No good, no good, no good." I felt like it was impossible to satisfy them. After three or four months, I had made over 200 that were all rejected. When I finally did make a good one ... Jiro said, "Now this is how it should be done." I was so happy I cried. It was a long time before Jiro referred to me as a shokunin. I wanted to say, "You just called me a shokunin, didn't you?" I was so happy that I wanted to throw my fist into the air! But, I tried not to let it show. That's what you strive for after all these years.

Shokunin means "artisan" and constitutes Jiro's highest expression of affirmation. It merits watching the film to see Nakazawa's face as he tells the story. Clearly, Jiro's praise is not simply a pat on the back for a job well done. Nakazawa achieved superior technical skills, but more importantly, he embraced an existential calling to be the best for the welfare of others. His accomplishment reflected the unrelenting pursuit of excellence, but it also manifested a spiritual calling that defined who he had become. Nakazawa cannot contain the inexpressible joy on his face.[16]

Is this not the transformational influence we want to have on those we lead, parent, teach, or coach? *Extraordinary Influence* seeks to bring out the best in the important people in our lives.

I've worked as a consultant in hundreds of organizations, and it is my strong opinion that the corporate world has not well integrated the benefits of affirmation. I've met some leaders who were notable exceptions; however, the considerable benefits of affirmation have not been harvested in most organizations I've observed. For that matter, few teachers, coaches, and even parents have put the power of transformational affirmation to work. Pats on the back and some "good jobs" are given, but nothing that gets to the core of the person.

> *In most organizations, the methods used to provide feedback to employees, such as performance appraisal or multi-rater feedback systems, often accomplish directly the opposite of what was intended because the recipients unrelentingly focus on their deficits.*

Many organizations languish because the culture fosters a negative, critical atmosphere. Leaders have not intentionally created a culture that affirms and encourages. The *gotcha* mindset prevails where leaders consistently look for who is screwing up. I also see this mindset in consulting organizations, including several where I served. It's like the *disease model* in medicine, where doctors are trained to look at what's wrong with the patient. What's more disconcerting is the seeming delight that members of organizations manifest about the ways in which other departments are messed up. Fights between sales and operations or sales and marketing are legendary.

In most organizations, the methods used to provide feedback to employees, such as performance appraisal or multi-rater feedback systems often accomplish directly the opposite of what was intended because the recipients unrelentingly focus on their deficits. Brain science tells us that these methods tend to engage a natural *negativity bias*, which is hardwired in us all. In many respects, it also just seems easier to criticize. Our own natures naturally seem to gravitate this way.

Affirmation is simply not in the repertoire of many organizational leaders (and parents, teachers, coaches, and so on). When I see a task-driven manager who doesn't put stock in the soft skills, he or she seems to relish a persona defined by, "I'm tough, stern, hard-nosed, and I hold people accountable," whatever that means. I presume holding people accountable means there will soon be a day of reckoning.

This pronouncement is usually delivered with either an apocalyptic foreboding or a highly self-righteous tone: "I don't let my people get away with anything. I'm the type of manager that calls my people to account. I'm going to find the slackers one way or the other, and they will pay." I've also noticed that these managers possess the right kind of frown. It's a cross between nervous fretting and the feigned somberness of a funeral director. It may sound like I'm describing Scrooge in *A Christmas Story*, but I'm not making this up. I hear these managerial pronouncements even in organizations that pride themselves on having a positive culture.

Of course, we must fix problems in our organizations (and get kids to accept age-appropriate responsibilities), but as we will learn in subsequent chapters, there are methods to engage parts of the brain that are inherently better at problem solving and innovation. Great leaders work hard at not tapping into the negativity bias inherent in our brains and, instead, focus their energy on accessing the parts of our brains that make us innovative, better at solving problems, and more resilient. There is a clear case for discussing and remedying the behavior of followers who are out of alignment with the goals we've set, but we now have irrefutable evidence that how we bring about alignment makes a huge difference in the motivation and effectiveness of workers.

Affirmation cannot fix every problem or heal every broken person.

It is also strikingly clear that in some instances, certain employees simply do not belong in an organization. I've been working with an electronic parts company's leadership team for many years. One member was so disruptive and created so much turmoil on the team that I strongly recommended the organization help her to leave. This recommendation followed several years of attempting to help the offending member become more self-aware and more self-governing. Despite my efforts, as well as those of the CEOs and some other team members, she would not change. The team approached me outside the usual meeting I normally attended to ask how they might precipitate her being fired. They felt her disruptive behavior had become so egregious and her work so incompetent and unethical that they were stupefied she had not been fired already. Several threatened to leave the company because they felt they could not stand working another day with the person in question. Several even speculated cynically that she must have some dirt on senior management. Otherwise, she surely would have been fired. I wondered the same thing! It is important to acknowledge early on that affirmation cannot fix every problem or heal every broken person.

Affirmation—The Means to Influence

This book is about how extraordinary influence can bring out the best in others. Let's establish at the beginning that positive influence is the outcome we seek. Affirmation is the means by which we achieve that influence. If we want to exert extraordinary influence and bring out the best in those around us, we must master the art of affirmation. We must learn how to affirm individuals, teams, and even whole organizations. We must also learn how affirmation can help someone on the fast track and the underperformer.

The last time I checked, there was an unlimited supply of affirmation available. It's not like we have to ration it.

My hope is that we might even infuse more affirmation into our society. Divisiveness today seems overwhelming. Imagine if our political leaders affirmed more. Imagine if the professional commentators affirmed even the leaders with whom they have strong differences in political views. What if we had more affirmation in our families, our classrooms, and our religious organizations. While I disavow any Pollyannaish notions that affirmation will cure all of society's ills, wouldn't we be healthier as a society if an atmosphere of affirmation was woven into the fabric versus the constant bickering and harangue of negativity?

The last time I checked, there was an unlimited supply of affirmation available. It's not like we have to ration it. It would make those around us healthier, more innovative, and just plain happier if it were shared more freely.

Most of the affirmation I express to others addresses people with whom I work, my clients, my family, and people I seek to encourage in my sphere of influence. The opportunities for affirmation and the people we affirm can also be quite random. Anne and I had a particularly excellent server when we went out to dinner recently. We affirmed him and thanked him for his excellent manner (we also told his manager). The server's voice became a bit husky as he acknowledged our affirmation. Recently, I had occasion to affirm a painter doing some work for us. I affirmed him because he does what he commits to do, and he meets our agreed upon deadlines. As I thanked him for his integrity, his eyes became watery.

We have a crosswalk at the Atlanta airport I use frequently and have almost been hit several times by cars speeding past the pedestrian crossing stop sign. I told the new police officer how much I appreciated her firm manner and for taking control of the crosswalk. She smiled broadly. While I don't mean to suggest that I am a paragon of virtue, it occurred to me that we can actually change our part of the world through this simple practice. Please, affirm away!

The task ahead is to learn how affirmation works. Imagine if we could all speak Words of Life as the coach did to my son!

Notes

1. http://www.etymonline.com/index.php?allowed_in_frame=0&search=affirmation.

2. Note to reader: Much of the research addresses the benefit of self-affirmation. By interference, experts acknowledge that these findings have value when considering other sources of affirmation.

3. J. D. Creswell, W. T. Welch, S. E. Taylor, D. K. Sherman, T. L. Gruenewald, and T. Mann, "Affirmation of Personal Values Buffers Neuroendocrine and Psychological Stress Responses," *Psychological Science* 16, no. 11 (2005): 846–851.

4. D. B. Sherman, D. P. Bunyan, J. D. Creswell, and L. Jaremka, "Psychological Vulnerability and Stress: The Effects of Self-Affirmation on Sympathetic Nervous System Responses to Naturalistic Stressors," *Health Psychology* 28, no. 5 (2009): 554–562.

5. J. D. Creswell, J. M. Dutcher, W.M. Klein, P. R. Harris, and J. M. Levine, "Self-Affirmation Improves Problem-Solving under Stress," *PLOS One* 8, no. 5 (2013).

6. O. Bartra, J. T. McGuire, and J. W. Kable, "The Valuation System: A Coordinate-Based Meta-Analysis of BOLD fMRI Experiments Examining Neural Correlates of Subjective Value, *Neuroimage* 76 (2013): 412–427, doi:10.1016/j.neuroimage.2013.02.063.

7. C. N. Cascio, M. B. O'Donnell, F. J. Tinney, Jr., M. D. Lieberman, S. E. Taylor, V. J. Strecher, and E. B. Falk, "Self-Affirmation Activates Brain Systems Associated with Self-Related Processing and Reward and Is Reinforced by Future Orientation," *Social Cognitive and Affective Neuroscience Advance Access* (2015).

8. B. J. Schmeichel and K. Vohs, "Self-Affirmation and Self-Control: Affirming Core Values Counteracts Ego Depletion," *Journal of Personality and Social Psychology* 96, no. 4 (2009): 770–782, doi:10.1037/a0014635.

9. These findings are supported by inference from: S. Achor, "Positive Intelligence: Three Ways Individuals Can Cultivate Their Own Sense of Well-Being and Set Themselves Up to Succeed," *Harvard Business Review* 90, no. 1–2 (2012): 100–102.

10. C. N. Cascio et al., "Self-Affirmation Activates Brain" (2015).

11. E. B. Falk et al., "Self-Affirmation Alters the Brain's Response to Health Messages and Subsequent Behavior Change," *Proceedings of the National Academy of Sciences USA* 112, no. 7 (2015): 1977–1982, doi:10.1073/pnas.1500247112.

12. C. K. W. De Dreu, "Oxytocin Modulates Cooperation within and Competition between Groups: An Integrative Review and

Research Agenda, *Hormones and Behavior* 61, no. 3 (2012): 419–428, doi:http://dx.doi.org/10.1016/j.yhbeh.2011.12.009.

13. R. E. Boyatzis, M. L. Smith, and N. Blame, "Developing Sustainable Leaders through Coaching and Compassion," *Academy of Management Learning and Education* 5, no. 1 (2006): 8–24.

14. G. L. Cohen and D. K. Sherman, "The Psychology of Change: Self-Affirmation and Social Psychological Intervention, *Annual Review of Psychology* 65 (2014): 333–371, doi:10.1146/annurev-psych-010213-115137.

15. http://www.magpictures.com/jirodreamsofsushi/.

16. http://adriancheok.info/uncategorized/secret-for-innovation-the-shokunin-spirit-of-japan/.

Part II
How Extraordinary Influence Works

3 Tactical Affirmation

Affirming Style and Competence

A few years ago, I spoke to a group of leaders who gathered in Izmir, Turkey, on the Aegean coast, a beautiful and archeologically rich area. Marc Antony and Cleopatra reportedly met for weekend getaways in nearby Ephesus. Because I was a speaker, my photograph appeared on some posters around the hotel to create awareness of my upcoming talks.

I'm allergic to dust, so I often leave a note for the housekeepers any time I stay for more than one night in a hotel. My note politely asks the housekeeper to leave the bedspread off the bed when the room is cleaned. I know it sounds a little particular, but bedspreads are magnets for dust; and, just between me and you, I don't like my imagination to get hold of what else might be on that bedspread from people sitting there, suitcases, and whatever else. So, I left my typical note to housekeeping: "Please leave the bedspread off the bed." Problem solved.

That night, my wife, Anne, and I had dinner with three other couples attending the conference. As we chit chatted about everyone's day, one of the wives spoke up and asked, "Did they make up your room today? Our bedspread wasn't even put back on the bed." Two others spoke up and said, "Weird, ours weren't, either."

I suddenly realized that the housekeeping staff must have seen my photo and thought that I was one of the conference organizers. They somehow took my note as a request to leave the bedspreads off all the beds in our group! We booked over 400 rooms in the hotel, and later that evening, I learned that a supervisor directed all the housekeepers not to put bed spreads *on any* of our conferees' beds when they cleaned the rooms!

As Anne and I were getting ready for bed that night, I said, "Well, you probably had no idea how powerful and influential your husband is." She said, "Actually, I just don't think they understand English!"

Fortunately, I have a very smart wife, who has a great sense of humor. She also knows when to rein in my eccentricities. "I like to think of myself as definitive—I'm clear about I want and communicate it appropriately." She said, "No, you're just picky."

We all have characteristics that define us. As I think about it, maybe I am a little picky. Whatever the characteristics of our style, we tend to act in fairly customary and predictable ways that people who know us or work with us come to expect. Have you ever noticed how some people can express a contrary thought in a conversation, and it benefits the discussion? Another person can express virtually the same contrary thought, but it feels adversarial and unhelpful. This is about style.

Affirmation must be thoughtfully guided to reach three dimensions in the human psyche.

If affirmation can powerfully influence another—a subordinate at work, a child, a student, a player on our team—how does it work? Affirmation must be thoughtfully directed to three dimensions in the human psyche, which makes any transformative influence we might exert with another person more effective. Affirmation varies according to the three dimensions or three faces shown in Figure 3.1.

1. **Customary Style**—those observable patterns that consistently characterize us. Our style determines **how well others receive us and our ideas.**

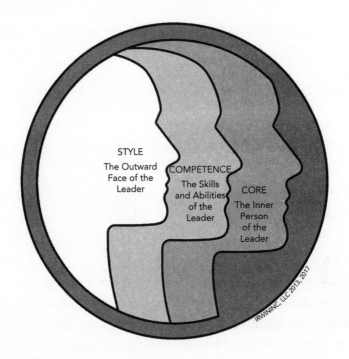

STYLE
The Outward
Face of the
Leader

COMPETENCE
The Skills
and Abilities
of the
Leader

CORE
The Inner
Person
of the
Leader

IRWININC, LLC 2013, 2017

Figure 3.1 Three Faces of a Leader

2. **Competence**—our skills, abilities, and knowledge behind effective actions. Our competencies determine **what we are able to do**.

3. **Core**—our inner person—the leader inside us. Our core determines **who we are—our character.**

Any leader who seeks to bring out the best in others affirms them in each of these three areas, but how and when varies significantly. Affirmation of our style and competence belong in the category of *tactical influence*. These dimensions are the ground level, daily, transactional initiatives we use to do our jobs. Leaders use affirmation day-to-day, week-to-week.

Affirming someone's core is *strategic influence*. By strategic, I mean far reaching, deeper, transformational, and overarching. Strategic influence potentially changes those we lead in their inner person. Leaders use affirmation less frequently and more opportunistically.

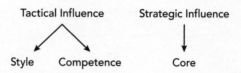

Figure 3.2 How Tactical and Strategic Influence are Applied

Figure 3.2 summarizes the differences between tactical and strategic influence.

As we established earlier in the book, *affirmation comprises the best way to influence those we lead,* but the *content* of the affirmation is quite different depending upon whether we affirm someone tactically or strategically. Great leaders create an intentional culture of affirmation using the appropriate content of tactical and strategic affirmation. This chapter considers the importance of tactical influence (affirmation of our style and competence). Chapter 4 describes strategic influence (affirmation of our core). A healthy, well-functioning organization (or a family or a team) needs both tactical and strategic influence. Both must be a part of the fabric of our organizational culture to bring out the best in those we lead.

How Do We Affirm the Style of Those We Seek to Influence?

A man who needed a job found an intriguing position listed on an organization's website, which read, "Must love animals and acting skills are a plus." The man e-mailed his resume declaring his devotion to animals and touting his lead role in a high school drama club play. To his surprise, the hiring organization was the local zoo and called him immediately. The zoo's starring attraction, a gorilla, needed surgery. He would be in recovery for a number of weeks, so the zoo wanted to dress up a man in a gorilla suit to see if they could fool the public for a month or two while the real gorilla recuperated. The man needed work and took the job. When he put on the gorilla suit, it was passable if you didn't get too close.

To the man's surprise, he actually enjoyed the work. It was not too stressful, and he had many adoring fans. One day, an especially large crowd gathered in front of his cage, and the gorilla decided to become a bit more daring. He planned to swing from one trapeze hung above his cage, do a summersault in midair and grab the trapeze on the other side of the cage, just like the acrobats in the circus. Because he had never done anything like this before, he misjudged the distance and threw himself so far when he let go of the first trapeze that he actually went up into the air and over the wall of the adjacent cage.

To his horror, the gorilla/man landed in the lion's cage, and the huge lion was extremely agitated, running back and forth in his cage roaring and shaking his bushy head in protest. People screamed for the zoo official to intervene in what promised to be a real live *Alien vs. Predator* battle. Suddenly, the lion swung around and stalked directly toward the interloper. Just as the gorilla was about to scream for help, the lion leaned over and said, "Shut up you fool, or we'll both be fired!"

We all wear some kind of suit—a gorilla suit, a lion suit, a bear suit, a giraffe suit, or any number of other suits. The suit we wear is our customary style, which defines us in fairly consistent ways others come to expect. It's how we come across to others. "He's intense," or "She's quiet." "She's a bit brusque." "His enthusiastic style is infectious." "He is quirky." "She's easy going." One manager I work with has a "terminal case of certainty." Never in doubt, he speaks with great authority even when there is no basis. His "I'm a great authority on all subjects" style is off-putting.

Style and Receptivity

Our style exerts a huge impact on how well we wear on others. Most importantly, it determines how others receive us and our ideas. For example, I tend to be a bit serious and introspective, so if I'm not careful, others can experience me as aloof or unfriendly. Nobody likes an aloof, unfriendly person, and, if I come across that way, it diminishes their receptivity to me. I'm generally a warm and caring person, but my serious style potentially obscures the warm side. I try to remind myself to smile at the people with whom I'm talking. Smiling helps that warmth break through, and ideally, makes others more receptive to me and my ideas. Self-awareness helps us leverage our positive attributes and mitigate those characteristics that potentially compromise our effectiveness.

Our style also wraps around our abilities and skills—our competencies—and substantially determines how effectively those abilities can be deployed. We all know of inventors or research scientists who cannot relate to others. These individuals may be brilliant, but their style works as an impediment to others' acceptance of them and their ideas.

Conversely, style facilitates receptivity. A person's style helps others to be receptive to his or her recommendations. Several weeks ago, I told a CEO that his style inspired confidence and hope about the growth plans of the company. His goals for growth are credible, but his style created optimism. He communicated the financial goals clearly—basically, information. The CEO's manner made his communication uplifting.

Think about four possible ways we might say, "No" to a subordinate who wants to pursue a new marketing initiative.

1. "This is a very creative, out-of-the-mainstream idea. We've been in a rut and really need this kind of breakout concept. My only question is whether the timing is quite right to put this in front of the executive team. I'll try to get a better read on when might be the optimal time to start socializing your idea. Let's keep this on low simmer for now—really appreciate your initiative and innovative thinking."

2. "I'm not interested in pursuing that idea now—maybe in the fall."

3. "You will have zero buy-in from anybody to pursue this."

4. "Pursuing that idea is a complete waste of time, and it would never fly with the CEO."

The action required in all four answers is essentially the same (postpone consideration), but the style is strikingly different (all four are real examples I've heard in meetings). My grandmother Goldie often said, "It's not what you say but how you say it." Responses 2 to 4 need some work if we're interested in bringing out the best in others!

> *To affirm the style of those we lead, we must develop a vocabulary of style.*

When someone affirms our style, it conveys recognition that it worked well in accomplishing a task, leading a team, or building a relationship. *Alliance Feedback*, the subject of Chapter 6, speaks to how we help someone whose style is out of alignment with their personal aspirations or the values and culture of the organization.

To make the idea of style practical and accessible, I provide four examples that I use in my work with senior executives. It is not critical that we have any model of customary style, but I provide this one as a point of reference. When we identify these characteristics in those we lead, there is great value in recognizing and affirming our follower's style, particularly when those distinctions add value and contribute to the success of our endeavor. *To affirm the style of those we lead, we must develop a vocabulary of style.* As in most areas of human behavior, our customary style contains a light and a dark side.

The four types of style—doer, advocate, idealist, and challenger—include characteristics that tend to wear well with others as well as those that interfere with effectiveness. Examples of affirming statements for each one are also included.

Doer—Customary style: Uses focused action to accomplish tasks

Upsides

Practical

Organized

Focused

Rational

Uses facts and experiences as reference points.

Possible Downsides

Lack of attention to the interpersonal dimension—can be insensitive

Low on passion

Low on creativity

Displays disrespect for those who lack technical skills and logic

Inflexible

Typical Affirmations

"Thank you for your focus on meeting the deadline."

"Thank you for bringing the discussion back to the real issues."

Advocate—Customary Style: Uses consideration of those most affected by decisions and inclusion/involvement of the major stakeholders

Upsides

Attention to people and their needs

Practical help for people

Inclusive

Loyal

Trusting

Commitment to relationships and the team

Sincerity, care, service, and support

Possible Downsides

Lack of attention to the task accomplishment

Naïve

Lacks decisiveness on tough people decisions

Lacks logic and analysis

Lacks focus on results

Typical Affirmations

"Thank you for encouraging the team today."

"You really drew Jenny into the discussion."

Idealist—Customary Style: Uses inspiring values and ideals to guide strategic initiatives

Upsides

Expresses guiding values that inspire us

Creative

Persuades with uplifting words and ideals

Passionate

Motivating

Contagious enthusiasm

Possible Downsides

Long on inspiration but short on attention to implementation

Impractical

Prone to champion ideals that have not been vetted

Gets lost in effusive words

Impatient with those who want to delve into the details

Accentuate their virtues without honest attention to their weaknesses

Typical Affirmations

"Your presentation really inspired our group to raise the bar on what we do for the field reps."

"Your reminder of the guiding values of our team helped us make a better decision today."

Challenger—Customary Style: Uses a challenging style to push through barriers and to prompt innovation and excellence

Upsides

Disrupts the status quo

Stretches boundaries

Goal clarity

Reminds us of mission and purpose

Attention to the goal and challenge

Possible Downsides

Impatience with those who don't immediately embrace the new ideas

Overbearing— "I know I'm right about this."

Not open to new ideas they did not originate

Intimidating

Can stifle creativity of others

Lack of appreciation for those not as conceptually grounded

Typical Affirmation

"You really helped us break out with some new thinking today."

"You quickly identified the real problem and the best solution."

While no model describes others perfectly in every situation, we do have fairly consistent ways in which we work and relate to others. To bring out the best in others we must seek to affirm those qualities that help our followers maximize their effectiveness. Our style, or the "suit" we wear, plays a vital part in determining the effectiveness of our actions.

We can even see these tendencies early in our children's lives. Our sons both displayed characteristics in grade school and adolescence that are still quite observable in adulthood—certain fundamental aspects of their behavior, that we might think of as style. As they matured through college and young adulthood, their styles became even more distinctive and increasingly effective as a way of relating to others.

Leaders should affirm subordinates' style when it makes them skilled at their work. In chapters 6 and 10, we will see how a leader can draw the person into alignment when the darker side of their style diminishes their work performance.

Competence

Tactical affirmation also includes the competence, or the source of actions for good or bad in those we seek to influence. Affirming their competence provides us with the opportunity to bring out the best in those we seek to influence.

Recently, an accounting manager in a manufacturing company told me about how he had blown an interaction with his boss. It was an obvious failure of *judgment*—a vital competency in the workplace. The manager clumsily introduced a subject that had nothing to do with the stated purpose of their meeting. The feedback to his boss was poorly timed, and worse, his comments made his boss feel like he was questioning an important recommendation the boss made to the CEO of their company. The boss became quite irritated and was aloof and distant toward the subordinate for the next month or so.

Over breakfast, the accounting manager who acted imprudently and I debriefed the meeting. The boss tends to be insecure, thin-skinned, and defensive in general. The subordinate knew that and realized he had blown the opportunity to build the personal trust level with his boss. We talked about how he could get back in good standing, and he concluded that he needed to apologize for mishandling the communication. He recognized that his own need to get the un-planned topic off his chest clouded his judgment and precipitated his impulsive action. "I couldn't wait," he said, "and impulsively waded into what I knew to be a volatile topic. In hindsight, I realized I could wait and should have waited until there were more favorable conditions." It took several months of effort but there was finally a thaw in the relationship. I affirmed his persistence in repairing the relationship and his determination to learn from his mistake, but also, we focused on listening to the caution that he should have heeded in the first place.

A paraphrase of an ancient king says, *Do you see someone skilled in their actions; he or she will end up at the top of the organization.*[1] Our competencies, like judgment, make a huge impact on our success in work and in life. Praising the competence of anyone we seek to lead is vital.

The following examples describe a random assortment of important competencies:

- Clearly communicates the vision
- Builds a strong and healthy team
- Fosters strong ethical commitments among subordinates
- Manages conflict skillfully

- Develops a viable succession plan to fill key roles across the organization
- Initiates cross-functional collaboration with appropriate balance between inclusion and efficiency in decision-making
- Creates an intentional, well-planned development process for the organization's emerging leaders
- Fosters a culture of work/life balance consistent with the organization's stated values
- Builds a healthy and uplifting culture
- Creates alignment on the team with goal clarity
- Takes personal responsibility for the organization's performance
- Builds trust in your critical relationships
- Makes timely decisions
- Fosters innovation
- Monitors key metrics
- Listens to input from peers
- Avoids political missteps
- Collaborates cross-functionally
- Hires strong contributors
- Continually learns and grows
- Motivates team members
- Manages ambiguity

Competencies like the ones above provide the foundation for what we are able to do. Like style, affirmation of the competencies our subordinates employed in their work provides a platform for influence. A number of CEOs I interviewed in connection with this book spoke with me about how to affirm the work of our subordinates. These recommendations are summarized in the following five guidelines for effective affirmation and include some examples.

1. *Show appreciation for the competencies underneath the actions.* Much of performance feedback in organizations concerns specific accomplishments. "The financial metrics look great." "You reached your sales goal." "You grew the EBITDA 5 percent over last quarter." "The new sales analyst you hired is an excellent fit with the job and our team." While noting specific accomplishments should be done, the competencies underneath the accomplishments should also be strongly affirmed. "You built a strong sales team, which is performing at the highest levels. The numbers are a result of your hard work in leading your team to collaborate with other departments to better serve our clients."

2. *CEOs recommended accomplishments be affirmed but also kept in context—why it mattered at the time.* "The board believes we must complement our strong performance in the high-end market with some mid-tier products. The brand analysis your team completed recently actually made the case the board needed to move into that market. Our CEO leveraged your data to justify the investment. Your excellent research and the compelling way you presented it helped accelerate this step by, at least, 18 months."

3. *Affirmation must be timely—real time.* "I heard from the West Coast office this afternoon. They said your implementation of the new systems went so smoothly, the team is in disbelief. Everyone thought the sales/operations divide would torpedo the effort. They're all happy and so are we!"

4. *Trust must precede feedback particularly if the feedback is contrary.* "Normally, you handle conflict extremely well. I understand the meeting with operations went off on a tangent and people got pretty frustrated. You know that I trust your handling of these things—I've been abundantly clear about that. I think you and operations should take another run at the impasse by the end of the week. You and Joe might set up some guardrails to keep the meeting on track next time."

5. *Affirmation must emanate from an authentic place when feedback is given.* "We disagreed on whether the market was ready for this type of investment product. I had serious doubts about it. You honored my reservations and gave more than ample attention to my concerns. You have a backlog of trust with me, and how you approached this continues to foster trust. Even though I'm still a bit queasy about the risks, I want you to proceed. I'm cheering for you and will do anything I can to help this effort succeed."

Affirming the competence of a subordinate creates a powerful opportunity for influence. John Pepper tells the story of when he made a huge mistake. He invested in a new product at P&G that his boss thought was a poor bet. It was. John went in to his boss's office knowing fully that he would be fired. He'd lost millions of dollars on a new product that nobody wanted. He told his boss about expecting to be fired, and his boss fired back, "Fired, what do you mean? We just invested $10 million in your training program." A number of years later, Pepper became CEO of P&G. Imagine the affirmation Pepper received in that experience. "Yes, you did a really bone-headed thing in creating that terrible product, but we value your abilities and even risk taking." He also learned some humility.

Why Affirm

We must never lose sight of the *why* of affirmation. It is the way to influence others and bring out the best in them. We start with the premise that people want to do a great job. They want to be successful. When that premise is in doubt, we may have the wrong person in the job. While this book addresses mainly organizational topics, the principles apply much more broadly.

A coach might say to a player, "You played a great game and kept their left tackle out of our backfield all night." A teacher might say,

"You worked hard this year and demonstrated an excellent grasp of AB level calculus. I want you to be in AP math next fall." A parent might say, "I'm really proud of you for being so organized. You're getting all your school assignments completed on time. Way to go!"

Affirmation implants beliefs into the core of those we want to influence, as we discussed in Chapter 2. These beliefs form a set of expectations. When a boss affirms a worker's style or competence, he or she grows in the conviction, "I am competent. I can do this." When new or more challenging circumstances arise, the affirmed person acts in concert with these beliefs.

Regrettably, the converse is true. Imagine a child who's been diminished by a critical parent over a long period of time. We can only imagine the beliefs formed in her core. "I'm stupid. I'm ugly. I can't get along with others." When I was a child, a popular girl a few years older than me frequently called me "Dummy." Why I even cared what she thought is beyond me, but I didn't have the self-confidence to ignore her. It took me a long time to replace that belief and begin to see that I could excel in school and in life. We have the privilege of strengthening those around us and implanting positive, uplifting beliefs in their cores. That's how we can have extraordinary influence!

Chapter 4 speaks to the most powerful type of affirmation. It is truly transformational.

Note

1. Proverbs 22:29, author's paraphrase.

4 Strategic Influence

How to Give Words of Life

For some years, I've worked with a manufacturing company in the southwestern United States. The company founder and CEO's middle daughter, Sally, took over as CEO when her father died a few years ago. Her two sisters had no interest in working at the company. Sally's dad epitomized the high-control type of leader. He made every decision from large capital expenditures to what type of coffee they drank in the break room.

Sally knew a lot about running manufacturing operations but she did not know the whole enterprise. When she took over, the first two years were stay the course—almost a grieving period. She made minimal changes and didn't even occupy her father's office. It stayed vacant almost like a memorial to him. Everyone wondered if she would ever put her own imprint on the company or simply try to continue to operate within the lines her father had drawn.

Sally worried that the changes she was contemplating might actually harm the company and that people wouldn't shift their allegiance to an untested new family member as CEO. She asked me to be an independent sounding board for the changes she wanted to make.

The business had been very successful, but it had also grown to the point where one person could not effectively control the company via force of personality as her father had done. The advent of ecommerce and internal management complexities required major rethinking of how to run the business. She also felt that some of the senior managers were not squarely behind her.

Over the next 12 months, Sally initiated some major changes, including parting ways with some of the old guard. She also reorganized the senior management team and worked on empowering managers at lower levels to make more decisions. While this might sound minor in scale to many seasoned leaders, it was a huge transformation for this company's culture.

Not without some significant hiccups, the business adapted well to the new cultural mandates and began growing new sales channels, a critically needed initiative. Sally's leadership changes created considerable stress and included significant financial risk. One morning as we ended a private meeting, I said to her, "Sally, I've worked with many companies, and very few CEOs have brought about the number of changes you have so skillfully. You have exhibited great integrity in the way you've handled some of the difficult personnel changes, always maintaining people's dignity publically and privately. You paid a significant emotional price to run the company differently than your father did. You demonstrated profound courage and initiative in making these changes. You faced down some important detractors and bumped heads with some big egos who sometimes patronized you. You went toe-to-toe with the banks to convince them that you were up to running the whole company. Your emotional resilience amazed everyone."

At that point, I stopped talking. As I observed Sally's face, she seemed almost hypnotized. Tears welled up. She said nothing for about a minute and then quietly thanked me for the encouragement.

What happened in that brief transaction? I spoke Words of Life to Sally's core. I had the privilege of observing her for many months as she navigated these difficult changes. What I was not doing was giving her a pat on the back and saying, "Good job." Rather, I affirmed the person inside her core. When this exchange happens authentically, the effect is almost magical. Affirmation of another's core manifests a power like no other. When skillfully and authentically delivered, Words of Life leave the recipient momentarily speechless.

Sally could not have gone through what she did without significant doubt. She took major risks with her company to bring about such wholesale changes. These Words of Life transformed her in that they deeply affirmed the courage and integrity she demonstrated in how she led the company.

While there had been other times over the months when I affirmed Sally's style, her competence, and her decisions, this represented a unique opportunity to affirm her in a more substantive way. It happened somewhat spontaneously but the thoughts had been in formation for some period of time. This is not something I would do every week, but when timed well, it transforms. I could see in Sally's face that she was lodging deeper convictions in her core about the type of leader she wanted to be going forward. My affirmation merged with a growing body of self-affirming statements. "I can do this. I can make good decisions. My instincts about where the company needs changing are right. I can figure out who's going to be on my team and those who cannot make the transition. I know I need others to help me run the company. I am growing in my confidence but I also know others must step up to lead." Her self-affirmation and the affirmation of others, including the words I spoke to her, lodged a growing set of beliefs in her core that would direct her going forward. Brain science now confirms that self-affirmation opens the pathway for others to speak into a person's core—more on this in Chapter 5.

In Chapter 3, we talked about affirming style and competence. These are critically important in the development of personal effectiveness; however, to truly bring about personal transformation, we must reach a person's core with Words of Life—the subject of this chapter.

Was I personally responsible for Sally's transformation? Absolutely not, but as a trusted advisor, I was a catalyst to encourage her to make the changes she knew were needed. I helped her codify the beliefs that were well underway in their formation.

When we are in a position of influence as an advisor, leader, parent, or coach, we can help the other person transform. We are, in fact, feeding the brain regions that are receptive to this type of affirmation, which then produce the transformation Sally longed to make in her own core! I was simply a catalyst.

What Is Our Core and How Do We Reach the Core of Another Person?

Throughout this book, I use the word *core* as a metaphor for the person inside us. Our core includes what the ancients metaphorically referred to as our "heart" or "mind." Hebrew writers referred to our "inward parts." They viewed our core as the seat of our character, conscience, courage, thoughts, feelings, attitudes, desires, considerations, and volition.

Where is our metaphysical core located? Philosophers and theologians have debated this question over the centuries. The anatomical location of our core is not important for how we will talk about our core in this discussion. In fact, the more scientists learn about us points to the complexity and interworking of our heart, brain, and whole body in determining how we behave.

> *Throughout this book, I use the word* core *as a metaphor for the person inside us. Our core includes what the ancients metaphorically referred to as our "heart" or "mind."*

What I hold unarguable is that a *person* exists inside us, a living being I call our core. This inner person acts, feels, thinks, speaks, has desires, makes decisions, and has identity. Our core has a voice, which social scientists sometimes call *self-talk*. Whether we are aware of it, there is a steady conversation going on inside us, and when we learn to pay attention to that voice, the revelations about ourselves can be at least informative if not startling. Some experts believe that the number of words we speak to ourselves each day far exceeds the number of words we speak to others. I sometimes ask people if they talk to themselves. Although we all talk to ourselves, I am surprised at the number of people who are not aware of their inner voice (or, at least, will not admit they hear their inner voice).

Our core learns, forms opinions, and serves as the chief repository of our beliefs. What I strongly advocate for leaders is that their beliefs should be formed thoughtfully and intentionally. Regrettably, I see many leaders adopt certain beliefs without careful vetting. The worst candidates for beliefs flow into our core through media—TV, cable news, movies, and social media. We often absorb beliefs from these sources unconsciously.

Our beliefs provide a major governance factor in our behavior. When our beliefs are sound and true, they lead to effective leadership. When those beliefs are errant, and we act on those errant beliefs, the results can be catastrophic. Tiger Woods said in his infamous news conference following his wife's discovery of his multiple affairs, "I told myself I didn't have to follow the normal rules. I told myself I was entitled. I now know that I do have to follow the normal rules." Tiger tragically discovered the reality that when we act on untrue beliefs, we sometimes pay a terrible price of personal destruction.

In an earlier book (*Impact: Great Leadership Changes Everything*[1]), I describe in much greater depth how beliefs are formed and how we are at considerable risk for lodging errant beliefs in our core.

Beliefs Reside in Our Core

1. Beliefs direct our behavior.

2. Beliefs reside in our core—the inner person that originates self-talk, thinks, authors opinions, and decides.

3. Beliefs form in a variety of ways:

- ◆ Self-reflection
- ◆ Input from influential people in our lives—bosses, parents, teachers, coaches, religious authorities, etc.
- ◆ Peers
- ◆ Books we read
- ◆ Media—TV, movies, social media, etc.
- ◆ Celebrities
- ◆ Advertising

4. Not carefully vetting our beliefs places us at great risk for the adoption of false beliefs, which sometime sends us down a terrible path of personal destruction. We have to be our own sentry, guarding our core from adopting errant beliefs.

5. If not carefully vetted, false beliefs lodge in our core as easily as true beliefs.

6. Vetting our beliefs requires disciplined introspection and resolute honesty. To be effective, we must pluck out and discard those false beliefs before the roots grow deep.

7. Even when we challenge faulty beliefs, we have great capacity to rationalize those that are self-serving, leaving those *rational lies* free to influence our behavior in unhealthy ways.

8. Power, fame, wealth, and notoriety place us at great risk for arrogance. These forces weaken the protective walls of our core and make us vulnerable for the adoption of untrue and especially toxic beliefs such as:

  ♦ I am the smartest person in the room.

  ♦ I am not subject to the rules that govern most people.

  ♦ I am entitled.

  ♦ I am not accountable to others for my actions.

  ♦ I am irreplaceable to the enterprise.

9. When false beliefs get translated into actions, a tremendous risk of derailment follows.

10. Positive beliefs form the same way as negative ones. Just as false beliefs lodge in our core, affirmation plants positive beliefs in our core, which result in positive behavior. Someone says, "You displayed integrity in the way you handled that interaction, and it reflected very positively on you." Thus, a belief is formed: "I want to strive for integrity in all my actions." This belief then guides future actions.

11. Self-affirmation, that is, sending ourselves edifying messages as well as receiving affirmation from others whose views matter provide the primary means of forming positive beliefs.

While our style and competence are much more visible in our actions, our core is deeper, less observable, and less easily accessible. Style and competent actions play a pivotal role in our effectiveness; however, our core plays an even more impactful role in making us strong leaders. A strong core guides us toward extraordinary influence of others and an enduring legacy.

When our core is intact and congruent, others see us as authentic, humble, and trustworthy. When our core is compromised or conflicted, others experience us as arrogant, self-serving, and insecure. No matter how artful their style or competent their actions, every derailed leader I studied possessed a malfunctioning core—breached in some significant way.

Words of Life

If you want to know the primary message of this book, you've found it. *Words of Life transform us, because they speak the language of the core.* When we speak Words of Life to another, they reflect a special vocabulary giving us access to another's core. If we want to reach the core of a subordinate, one of our children, a student, or anyone else we seek to influence, we must give them Words of Life. By give, I mean give the other person a gift. Your words spoken authentically into their core will likely be the most important gift some people will ever receive. In my interviews with CEOs for this book, I was struck by how many reported what their boss said to them at critical junctures in their lives and how often their boss's words became an inflection point for good. Their bosses may not have known the phrase *Words of Life*, but nonetheless, they gave these future CEOs Words of Life at just the right time.

Words of Life contain the force to transform another person; they are significantly different from the words we might use to affirm another's style or competence. Words of Life truly bring out the best in another. Words of Life transform us and bring out the best in the important people we long to influence.

The act of affirming someone with Words of Life implants *redemptive beliefs* in a person's core, which, in turn, produces *redemptive actions*. By redemptive, I mean lifesaving, liberating, nurturing, and transformative.

Word of Life speak about our character—the unassailability of our inner person.

For example, when a vice president of marketing affirmed his manager for the courage and tact she skillfully displayed in telling the CEO that his business plan contained some seriously flawed assumptions, a belief took root in her core: *Risk-taking is not easy, but telling our CEO the truth was the right thing to do. I must convey respect and appreciation for others' work, while not holding back on explaining the flaws that could hurt the performance of our organization.*

What Are Words of Life?

What is the common thread in Words of Life? These powerful words speak about our character—the unassailability of our inner person. Words of Life address the dimensions of our core and speak the vocabulary of our core. The following list contains 10 types of affirmation that speak to another's core with an example in each category. These dimensions make it clear that Words of Life differ dramatically from a pat on the back.

My examples relate to what corporate leaders might say to people in their organization, but parents or teachers or coaches would use the same categories of core affirmation for those they seek to influence. I provide examples of age-appropriate Words of Life for children in Chapter 11.

Integrity

"When our manufacturing representative wanted us to sell our product to a country with a long history of human rights abuses and religious persecution, you made the call that we would not sell to them. This decision hurt your sales numbers and therefore your personal bonus for the year, but you showed tremendous integrity in that decision. I commend you."

Courage

"You knew the CEO badly wanted to acquire that company even if the deal had some 'hair' on it. When you became aware that they intentionally misstated their EBITDA, you stood up to her and said you could not in good conscience recommend to the board that we buy that company. I tremendously respect the courage that required. The CEO was upset because she wanted their product line anyway. Your courage gave others courage, and we did what we all knew we should do—pass on the deal."

Humility

"You've received a ton of great press for closing that huge development deal—even a mention in the *Wall Street Journal*! When you gave your acceptance speech at the awards banquet the other night, you handled the accolades very honorably. By mentioning each member of your team by name and the contribution each had made, you moved the attention off of you and on to those committed few who made the deal happen. Your humility and self-effacing manner endeared your team and the rest of us to you even more."

Judgment

"The conflict over how to state the earnings with our second largest customer had disaster written all over it. We knew and most of them knew our solution was right. You navigated this so skillfully and judiciously that the leader of their accounting department saved face, even though he was clearly in the wrong. It was truly a work of art to make him the hero. You demonstrated great judgment and probably made them a customer for life."

Authenticity

"Your team really respects and trusts you. I believe that results from being truthful and realistic with them. You don't try to manipulate them with rosy forecasts not grounded in reality. Your peers really trust you as well. They believe whatever you tell them is true. Your authenticity is a huge asset, and I wish more people followed your example.

Self-regulation

"You had every right to throw the whole legal department under the bus and run over them multiple times. You didn't do that, even though everybody at the meeting knew how badly they messed up the sale. Your restraint surprised us all when you could have really embarrassed them if you presented the details of how they torpedoed the deal to trump up their standing with the board. Even when the VP of legal tried to tarnish you, you didn't retaliate. The VP did himself no favors when he didn't own the problem. By the way, the CEO took the head of legal to the woodshed on Friday afternoon and made it clear that he knew exactly what happened. He also informed the Lead Director. You handled this really well."

Wisdom

"I have no idea how you figured out the solution, but you remedied that problem with extraordinary skill. The client was happy that you were able to solve what has been a vexing problem for at least five years. It required very skillful navigation among the company, the tax lawyers, and the IRS. I'm not sure anyone else here could have pulled that off. Our CEO and I are deeply grateful for your work."

Candor

"That was impressive! Nobody wanted to point out the dead cat under the table. It stunk but nobody wanted to say it was there. When you spoke up, it dramatically relieved the tension in the room. Your honesty and directness completely disarmed the strain we all felt and changed the direction we were headed. Most of us knew we were courting disaster, but someone had to speak up and label it for what it was. Thank you for saying what all of us should have said ourselves!"

Resilience

"You displayed great mental and emotional toughness over the last six months. The pace for all us of has been exhausting, but you manifested a special degree of persistence and flexibility over the entire length of the negotiation. Your tremendous stamina and good humor made this deal happen. Everybody in the C suite is ecstatic that we were successful, when odds-makers on the twentieth floor gave this deal a 1 out of 3 chance of closing. Thank you for an outstanding accomplishment."

Influence

"The CEO tried to force this change on the organization two years ago, and it got him fired—the rebellion he created justified his firing. Our financial results and our morale tanked. Oddly, what he wanted to do was the right thing. He just did such an awful job of trying to force everybody to get in line. You won people over with vision, your winsome manner, and very convincing financial analysis. Your involvement of so many stakeholders won the day. They shaped the solution and then became the sponsors of the change. You demonstrated great skill in moving this to completion with everybody on board. You should be proud of this noteworthy achievement."

Effective style and great competence are tremendously important, but when qualities of character are affirmed, we are much more likely to bring out the best in the person we seek to influence.

May I repeat this thought for emphasis. Words of Life affirm the qualities that can make our character unassailable. In most cases, leaders tend to affirm an action someone has taken. A far more powerful step is to affirm some dimension of a person's core which prompted the desired action. Effective style and great competence are tremendously important, but when qualities of character are affirmed, we are much more likely to draw out the best in the person we seek to influence.

Some leaders intuitively grasp this and use Words of Life. For others, it becomes a skill to master. In either case, Words of Life must authentically radiate from the core of the giver. One CEO I interviewed said, "The affirmation of another must come from inside you. It cannot be parroted. It must be authentic."

When skillfully and authentically delivered, Words of Life leave the recipient momentarily speechless.

When a relationship of trust exists, another person allows us unique access to his or her core. The Words of Life we give them flow into their core and contain great potential to transform the recipient for good. The likelihood is high that a parent, a coach, a teacher, a boss, or some other important person has spoken Words of Life to us. Those words lifted us by creating beliefs that changed us. Over time, our actions reflected the beliefs that lodged in our core.

A very close friend in college challenged me to a life of excellence. I wasn't actively pursuing mediocrity, but the trend line certainly was headed in that direction. In many conversations, he encouraged me to set a higher bar for my life—that I, in fact, could and should become a person of extraordinary influence. At the time, I did not consciously adopt those beliefs, but my friend's Words of Life lodged deep into my core and began to influence many major decisions and actions. I had no conscious awareness his words would prove to be so consequential. My life simply took a very different trajectory from the one I previously set. What I also experienced at the time felt more like renewal. An ancient proverb says, "Trustworthy messengers refresh like snow in summer. They revive the spirit … "[2]

Seven Not-So-Good Reasons to Avoid Expressing Words of Life

Perhaps we feel some resistance to expressing Words of Life to someone we lead. What are some possible reasons?

1. "I just don't think in those terms. I focus on the business to be done."

2. "It just feels too personal. It's awkward."

3. "I'm not a go deep kind of person. I'm just a shallow coper."

4. "I feel embarrassed about this kind of stuff."

5. "It could really backfire."

6. "I worry that HR will come after me for saying something too personal to an employee."

7. "I actually just don't care that much about people's feelings. I just want them to do their jobs."

Under What Conditions Can We Give Words of Life?

Leaders transform those around them through intentional affirmation of another's core. How do we best convey Words of Life?

- We must have an intact core ourselves. When we give Words of Life, they must originate in our core. If the walls of our core are breached through arrogance or some other compromise, we cannot reach the core of another.

- We must be authentic. Our affirmation must be true.

- Our words must be carefully considered. An ancient proverb says, "A word aptly spoken is like apples of gold in settings of silver."[3] Words of Life reach deep because they are thoughtful. Words of Life are not throw away lines!

- We must use the right vocabulary—Words of Life draw from the well of character. The examples mentioned previously include integrity, courage, humility, judgment, authenticity, self-regulation, wisdom, candor, resilience, and influence.

- Words of Life are conveyed upon a foundation of trust between the giver and the receiver.

- Words of Life may be given spontaneously or planned, as long as they are thoughtful and sincere.

- Words of Life must be given when the receiver is the sole focus at the moment.

Words of Life are a precious gift for the receiver. They may set a person's life in a whole new direction, as in my case. They may simply strengthen the receiver for the next major challenge he or she faces. Regardless, this powerful form of affirmation makes people feel alive, perhaps more so than ever.

My wife tutored children at an inner-city school in Atlanta for several years. Her experience at the school later led her to start a non-profit organization aimed at solving big problems in our city, for example, education and the development of young children who grow up without many advantages, such as being able to read a good book. Jarius, the young boy she tutored in reading, was several grade levels behind, but that day Jarius experienced a breakthrough. Anne said, "Jarius, you've worked so hard for all these months and now you're reading so well, I have some good news—you've caught up!" His eyes suddenly became bright, a huge smile flashed across his face, and in the most exuberant voice imaginable, he said, "Yes, I can read! I can read! I can read!" They both had a good laugh and a good cry in celebration of his accomplishment. Anne gave Jarius Words of Life that day and like all the other remarkable graduates of his school, eight years later he went on to college.

It is our great and unique privilege to bring out the best in others by giving them Words of Life.

Notes

1. Tim Irwin, *Impact: Great Leadership Changes Everything,* BenBella, 2014.
2. Proverbs 25:13 (New Living Translation).
3. Proverbs 25:11 (New International Version).

5 Words of Death

Constructive Criticism Fails Because Our Brains Are Hard Wired for Something Better

My wife, Anne, founded and leads a highly successful fine art gallery. Her gallery represents about 40 artists whose work is hung in many notable places. Yet, any interest she had in art was almost squelched when she was six years old. Her first-grade teacher, Ms. Caldwell, seemed like she was 100 years old to the children in her class. Every day she wore the big heel, lace up style black high-tops fashionable among older women at the time and the same ankle-length gray dress.

On Friday, the children had art class. Sally Young, clearly the teacher's pet, mastered the *sine qua non* of first grade art—house with curly gray smoke coming out of the chimney, blue sky, green grass, tree with rounded crest, cute squirrel on a low tree branch, and flowers in front of the house. Sally was most excellent at this traditional style of art.

Anne, a bored rebel, on an impulse began to flick her brush toward the big sheet of paper on the easel in an array of interesting colors and shapes. She was mesmerized when two colors merged to create a third. The dripping runs of paint made her art like no other. The class had a non-representational art prodigy in their midst—Anne was truly a budding Jackson Pollack at six years old. They were in the presence of greatness!

The unfortunate by-product of Anne's creativity was that some paint splattered on the floor. Crotchety Ms. Caldwell was incensed. She interrupted the class and reprimanded Anne in front of all the other students. "Look at the mess Anne has made." Anne felt such shame that she burst into tears, ran to her desk, and lay her head down sobbing. Lesson learned—play it safe, conform, and be like Sally Young.

Fortunately for other rising students with a creative bent, that was the year Ms. Caldwell retired, but the shame she dispensed so forcefully to Anne still resides in her core and even surfaces occasionally as a painful memory. In fact, brain science offers strong support for the theory that the shame she experienced is still stored in a specific location in her brain, probably even a particular neuron. If only there was a delete key for those kinds of memories.

I've sometimes had an imaginary conversation with Ms. Caldwell, Anne's first grade teacher. It's probably good that I cannot have that conversation, because it would likely go against the grain of much I will say in this book. I would like to ask her if she wants a redo of that conversation about Anne's splattering paint on the floor. How about, "Oh Anne, what a different and creative way to apply paint. I am so proud of you for exploring new ways to make interesting shapes and colors. Class, look at what Anne painted. Isn't this creative?" And then quietly, so none of the other children would hear, "Anne honey, be sure to wet some paper towels and clean up the spattered paint. Your new technique was a little messy, but that's okay. What a wonderful painting you made today!"

Words of Death

An ancient proverb says, "Words can bring death or life!"[1] Like many forces, words contain a duality, and the proverb starkly captures this distinction. In Chapter 2, I introduced the concept of Words of Life. Our words can build a stronger core in those we influence, or our words commensurately contain the power to weaken the core of someone we lead. Even if we possess an emotionally stalwart constitution, our spirit can still be crushed when we are the recipient of withering criticism, ridicule, or shame from an important other, such as a parent, a coach, a teacher, a peer, or a boss.

Our words can build a stronger core in those we influence, or our words commensurately contain the power to weaken the core of someone we lead.

This phenomenon fits with my concern that many managers, as a practical matter, mainly care about accomplishing tasks more so than showing interest in who we are as a person. When we give feedback to a subordinate absent concern about his or her person, we bypass the parts of the person's brain that powers innovation, problem solving, creativity, and self-worth. What's worse, as we will see in this chapter, we engage the part of the brain that shuts out any positive influence we might intend!

The Dirty Dozen—Why Criticism Is a Really Bad Practice

Scientific research provides an overwhelming amount of research on the negative effects of criticism on the well-being of followers. By inference, it's easy to say these studies apply as well to parents, teachers, coaches, and anyone who leads others. Here are 12 key findings from brain research about what happens when we diminish people with criticism.

1. Criticism engages our amygdala, the part of the brain that houses the "fight or flight" response. The amygdala also processes positive emotions, but it possesses a *negativity bias*, and goes on hyper alert to any perceived threat, including negative feedback from the boss or other important person.[2]

2. Higher order brain functions are severely disrupted when a person is diminished. During criticism, our brains have less access to some of the most positive resources of the brain, such as higher order thinking, self-reflection, creativity, problem solving, and stress regulation.[3,4,5,6] These effective coping resources shut down in the presence of strong criticism.

3. Similarly, during criticism, people's brains have dramatically reduced interconnectivity among higher order thinking, self-reflection, and stress regulation.[7]

4. During criticism, the recipient absorbs the negative emotions of the critic.[8]

5. Negative/critical leadership results in lower productivity, negative attitudes, and low satisfaction from employees. Abusive supervision leads to extreme negative consequences such as decreased creativity, productivity, commitment, and increased depression and anxiety.[9]

6. Critical feedback can be perceived as injustice in the workplace and leads to decreased productivity and commitment, and increased depression and anxiety. People resist critical leaders and have lower productivity and negative attitudes.[10]

7. Diminishing feedback from leadership leads to many negative mind and body effects. Abusive supervision not only causes psychological distress, but costs organizations financially.[11] These stress-induced health issues contribute to negative employee attitudes and work-performance problems. Not only are diminished employees less productive, they are also more likely to suffer additional health-care costs associated with sleep disturbance, depression, and anxiety.[12] Long-term chronic stress may even cause memory problems.[13] By inference, an employee working under long-standing harsh criticism would be expected to suffer memory problems, as well.

8. When employees don't see criticism as accurate and relevant to themselves, they become hostile and fail to see validity even when the feedback is applicable.[14]

9. Inconsistent and unpredictable support from a supervisor increases negative outcomes for employees.[15]

10. There is a trickle-down effect wherein abusive department leaders create abusive team leaders. Reduced productivity results.[16]

11. When an organizational culture routinely uses a threat of criticism and punishment for nonconforming behavior, creative insight and workers' attention spans diminish. Rigid conformity promotes more black and white thinking. Creativity and the resulting innovation to products and processes is lost.[17]

12. When a supervisor undermines the interpersonal dimension, it makes employees less happy and less committed, more aggressive and counterproductive. This reflects a

well-substantiated conclusion supported by the scientific
literature.[18]

What are the most important conclusions we might draw from the dirty dozen research studies?

There's something about criticism that we experience as
highly negative at a primordial level. Whether intended
or not, the recipient of critical feedback hears that it's not
what we did, but it's more about *who we are*. Disapproval
and disparagement from an important person sends us
a fundamental message that we're not okay. Criticism
diminishes our self-worth, and our brains react with
profound negativity.

Critical leaders may be unintentionally conditioning people
to respond in fearful or stressful ways. In the famous "Little Albert" study, baby Albert was classically conditioned
to fear a white rat. Fear conditioning was so effective that
eventually Albert generalized his fear and became afraid of
any small, white creature, such as a rabbit. Classical conditioning to fear a supervisor, such as when the boss displays
chronic dislike of a subordinate, can have long-term and
generalized effects. In this way, learning to fear or dislike a
bad boss may be generalized to dislike of the entire organization.

While undoubtedly, a critical supervisor intends to improve
productivity through his or her negative feedback, the
exact opposite occurs. The productive and creative parts of
our brains go into meltdown mode when harsh criticism
is delivered. Productivity suffers, psychosomatic illnesses
increase,[19] and workers are basically unhappy.

Criticism of a person and not an action particularly leads to decreased self-worth of employees. When managers care more about tasks than the needs of the worker, the negative impact is dramatically greater.

A manager's habitual use of criticism (Words of Death) rises to the level of abusive leadership, which leads to extreme negative consequences such as decreased creativity, productivity, and commitment, and increased depression and anxiety. What is worse than abusive criticism? *Inconsistent and unpredictable* support from a supervisor, because this style even further exaggerates negative outcomes for employees.[20,21,22] The hapless employee is then whipsawed by the constantly changing demeanor of an unpredictable boss. A key to happy and productive employees is a leader's consistently supportive behavior.

While undoubtedly, a critical supervisor intends to improve productivity through his or her negative feedback, the exact opposite occurs.

The Social Workplace

While we would likely consider our families a far more important tribe to which we belong, we still identify strongly with where we work. A lack of social connectedness at work, or anywhere else for that matter, can be devastating. Rejection from the tribe or getting voted off the island is processed in our brains in a similar way to physical pain and can even feel physically painful.[23]

Ms. Caldwell's dressing down of Anne was particularly outrageous because she berated her in front of the whole class. It was terrible that she spoke to a six-year-old in the manner she did, but to shame her in front of her peers was unconscionable. When I talk with leaders, I urge them to praise in public and correct in private. My redo for Ms. Caldwell illustrated how this might have gone dramatically better.

Whether intended or not, the recipient of critical feedback hears that it's
not what I did, but it's more about who I am.

Social conformity does not activate higher cognitive areas in
our brains, but rather activates an "emotional processing center."[24]
This brain region controls dopamine release, a very important brain
chemical, which facilitates our ability to feel good about our work.
This research suggests that being a part of a tribe is very rewarding
in and of itself. The important idea for us is that unbridled criticism
makes us feel like we've been expelled from the tribe.

This may also be why people are willing to go to such great lengths
to fit in. In the famous "Asch Conformity Experiment" (also known
as the "longest line" study), participants in a group setting viewed two
cards containing vertical lines. The first card contained one vertical
line. The second card displayed three vertical lines, labeled A, B, and
C. One of the three lines was the same length as the line on the first
card, and participants were asked to identify which one. A few of the
participants were confederates of the experimenter, and they gave what
was obviously the wrong answer. A majority of the other participants
then also gave the wrong answer. It was plainly obvious that people
wanted so badly to be part of the group, they repeated the wrong
answer to the experimenter.

Shame Speaks Words of Death

During the cratering of Anne's painting career, a particularly distress-
ing aspect was that she *didn't hear* Ms. Caldwell's Words of Death as
negative feedback about her style of art or even the fact that there was
splattered paint on the floor. Her extreme emotional reaction demonstrated this. *What Anne heard was that there was something wrong with
her.* This is often the source of shame, an even more powerful form of
diminishment. Anne risked an unbridled expression of her creativity,

departing from the socially accepted first grade norm of what constitutes good art. Creativity and personal risk-taking emerge from the core of who we are. When we are criticized for expressing something from our core, we receive the feedback as an impoverishment of our person. It goes straight to our self-worth.

As we will learn more specifically in Chapter 6, it was perfectly fine for Anne to be asked to take responsibility for cleaning up the splattered paint on the floor. In my imaginary redo, this was accomplished. What was not okay was the shaming and social ostracism that her teacher precipitated through her harsh criticism.

The Worst of All Legacies

Known as the *imprinting* phenomena, at a critical window in a very young animal's life, whatever it sees first becomes its *mother*. While in graduate school, a baby chicken imprinted on me and followed me everywhere I went in my back yard! Many times, leaders in various organizations told me that they learned to manage by mimicking their first boss's management style; we learn a lot from the example of those who lead us, particularly early in our careers—we imprint on them. Many CEOs I interviewed for this book stressed that they had very positive role models in the intervening years between when they started work and when they became CEO. In contrast, perhaps the worst consequence of a criticism-oriented manager is the modeling of a critical style to members of the organization with a high potential for future leadership responsibility.

Like a family unit, positivity and negativity are often carried on across generations. A negative leader is more likely to groom negative leaders under his or her charge.[25] Considerable risk exists that a follower will perpetuate a management style of criticism and negativity when the boss reflects that style. It is well known that parents who abuse their children often produce adults who abuse their children.

Negativity is contagious, so it perpetuates negativity among those over whom we have influence.

We have special "copy-cat cells" in the brain called "mirror neurons," which fire when we watch someone else's behavior.[26] Scientists believe mirroring might be the reason that we can be empathetic toward others. Unlike the mirrors in our homes, these mirrors in our minds travel with us everywhere, even to work! Mirror neurons might also underlie the findings of a recent study showing that peoples' brains automatically show a threat response when they simply *think* they might receive a shock.

Our moods are contagious, so it's important to reflect upon how our mood might affect others, and how others' moods affect us. We are natural copy-cats. We love to fit in to make others happy, as can be seen via the famous "Bobo Doll Experiment."

Perhaps the worst consequence of a criticism-oriented manager is the modeling of a critical style to members of the organization with a high potential for future leadership responsibility.

In this experiment, scientists observed that when an authority figure models a behavior, those under his or her influence perpetuate the behavior. Children watching a video of adults abusing a Bobo Doll with punches were much more likely to be aggressive to the Bobo Doll themselves. People truly learn by seeing, so bad behavior begets bad behavior.

Culture significantly influences our leadership behavior. An organizational culture that emphasizes structure, obligations, and punishments for deviant behavior further diminishes followers' creative insight and attention span.

Over the course of working in the corporate world for many years, I have seen countless examples of strong, positive cultures as well as many I would describe as toxic. One of the most toxic cultures I have observed is the "gotcha" style. Managers are expected to catch employees in a departure from rules or other standards. They seem to relish being the one who nails the perpetrator for even the most minor infraction. This fosters a negative, critical, and harsh culture in which people are constantly on edge.

Our personal psychological adjustment constitutes a major force in determining our effectiveness. A leader's poor psychological adjustment often contributes to a harsh and abusive style of leadership. I consulted with a heavy equipment manufacturer in the Midwest for a few years. To use one of my grandmother's homespun diagnoses, the CEO was a "mess." His emotional volatility intimidated everyone within shouting distance. His terminal case of certainty, despite mountains of evidence to the contrary, governed his leadership style. He was virtually un-coachable. I firmly believe the only reason people worked in his company was because he paid people well above market for their positions. Most of his senior team were one good offer from moving to another company.

The CEO asked me to help vet the talent at senior levels. At my urging, the CEO involved employees from several levels of the organization to help vet candidates for a new vice president of marketing. I recommended a process in which the five employees conducted a panel interview, and I gave them a few tips on how they could best work together to learn about the candidate. The panel ended up really liking one candidate and really disliking the other. During the debrief session, it became obvious that the CEO felt exactly the opposite from the panel regarding who was the stronger candidate. He told the panel very forcefully, "You're wrong!" The panel's enthusiasm and commitment to help vet the candidates dissipated immediately only to be replaced with anger and frustration at the CEO's harsh criticism. Several weeks later, when new information surfaced, it became obvious that the panel was exactly right about the two candidates!

Can a Leader's Fundamental Style Change to Become Less Critical?

I am often surprised when businesses tolerate abusive managers. Unfortunately, if they get results, they often get a pass for how they treat people. If enough people complain to HR, then that can tip the scales, but their behavior must be egregious.

What I'm about to say would be a source of disagreement among many experts. When a company asks me to work with an abusive manager to help him or her change their management style, I'm usually very reluctant to take on that assignment. The likelihood of success is very small, and offering a manager help may be more about assuaging the guilt of those making the ultimate firing decision. "Well, we tried to help Sam, but it's just in his DNA to treat people harshly. He'll never change."

Sometimes, these managers have a better chance of making it somewhere else, because their negative personal brand is too established in the organization. It is a psychological and financial benefit for companies to monitor and often remove abusive supervisors for the health and well-being of employees. I recommend a no-tolerance policy on abusive supervision.

The big question we ask from this chapter is if you can't criticize someone and tell them what's wrong, how can that person improve and get better? What's a great leader to do when members of his or her organization are not in alignment with the values, mission, goals, standards, and processes of the organization? How to correct poor performance is the subject of Chapter 6. There is a better way!

Join My Crusade

One of the phrases that we've heard all our lives is *constructive criticism*. What it usually means is that I'm going to gut you emotionally, but my motives are positive. There is usually nothing constructive about it and telling us in advance puts us on hyper alert. I've never heard of even one example where criticism was constructive. Have you?

Perhaps you've been looking for a cause to join. This is it. I propose a worldwide ban on the phrase *constructive criticism*. You can sign the petition on my website: www.drtimirwin.com. People of the world unite—eradicate the term *constructive criticism*!

Notes

1. Proverbs 18:21, Contemporary English Version (CEV), American Bible Society, 1995.

2. A. Etkin, T. Egner, and R. Kalisch, "Emotional Processing in Anterior Cingulate and Medial Prefrontal Cortex," *Trends in Cognitive Sciences* 15, no. 2 (2011): 85–93, doi:10.1016/j.tics.2010.11.004.

3. D. Liu, H. Liao, and R. Loi, "The Dark Side of Leadership: A Three-Level Investigation of the Cascading Effect of Abusive Supervision on Employee Creativity," *Academy of Management Journal* 55, no. 5 (2012): 1187–1212, doi:10.5465/Amj.2010.0400.

4. E. Miron-Spektor et al., "Others' Anger Makes People Work Harder Not Smarter: The Effect of Observing Anger and Sarcasm on Creative and Analytic Thinking," *Journal of Applied Psychology* 96, no. 5 (2011): 1065–1075.

5. M. N. Servaas et al., "The Effect of Criticism on Functional Brain Connectivity and Associations with Neuroticism," *PLOS One* 8, no. 7 (2013), doi:10.1371/journal.pone.0069606.

6. B. J. Tepper, "Abusive supervision in work organizations: Review, synthesis, and research agenda," *Journal of Management* 33, no. 3 (2007): 261–289. doi:10.1177/0149206307300812.

7. M. N. Servaas et al., "The Effect of Criticism."

8. D. Liu et al., "The Dark Side of Leadership."

9. M. K. Duffy, D. C. Ganster, and M. Pagon, "Social Undermining in the Workplace," *Academy of Management Journal* 45, no. 2 (2002): 331–351, doi:10.2307/3069350.

10. M. S. Mitchell and M. L. Ambrose, "Abusive Supervision and Workplace Deviance and the Moderating Effects of Negative Reciprocity Beliefs," *Journal of Applied Psychology* 92, no. 4 (2007): 1159–1168, doi:10.1037/0021-9010.92.4.1159.

11. B. J. Tepper, M. K. Duffy, C. A. Henle, and L. S. Lambert, "Procedural Injustice, Victim Precipitation, and Abusive Supervision," *Personnel Psychology* 59, no. 1 (2006): 101–123, doi:10.1111/j.1744-6570.2006.00725.x.

12. B. J. Tepper, "Consequences of Abusive Supervision," *Academy of Management Journal* 43, no. 2 (2000): 178–190, doi:10.2307/1556375.

13. B. S. McEwen, "Stress and Hippocampal Plasticity," *Annual Review of Neuroscience* 22 (1999): 105–122, doi:10.1146/annurev.neuro.22.1.105.

14. This conclusion is drawn by inference from a large body of scientific evidence.

15. M. K. Duffy et al., "Social Undermining in the Workplace."

16. D. Liu et al., "The Dark Side of Leadership."

17. C. K. W. De Dreu and B. A. Nijstad, "Mental Set and Creative Thought in Social Conflict: Threat Rigidity versus Motivated Focus," *Journal of Personality and Social Psychology* 95, no. 3 (2008): 648–661, doi:10.1037/0022-3514.95.3.648.

18. This a summary statement of the research cited for the Dirty Dozen.

19. D. Montano, "Supervisor Behaviour and Its Associations with Employees' Health in Europe," *International Archives of Occupational and Environmental Health* 89, no. 2 (2016): 289–298, doi:10.1007/s00420-015-1072-8.

20. B. Ashforth, "Petty Tyranny in Organizations," *Human Relations* 47, no. 7 (1994): 755–778, doi:10.1177/001872679404700701.

21. M. K. Duffy et al., "Social Undermining in the Workplace."

22. H. Hoel, L. Glaso, J. Hetland, C. L. Cooper, and S. Einarsen, "Leadership Styles as Predictors of Self-reported and Observed Workplace Bullying," *British Journal of Management* 21, no. 2 (2010): 453–468, doi:10.1111/j.1467-8551.2009.00664.x.

23. D. T. Hsu et al., "Response of the Mu-Opioid System to Social Rejection and Acceptance," *Molecular Psychiatry* 18, no. 11 (2013): 1211–1217, doi:10.1038/mp.2013.96.

24. M. Stallen, A. Smidts, and A. G. Sanfey, "Peer Influence: Neural Mechanisms Underlying in Group Conformity," *Frontiers in Human Neuroscience* 7 (2013), doi:10.3389/fnhum.2013.00050.

25. D. Liu et al., "The Dark Side of Leadership."

26. G. Rizzolatti and L. Craighero, "The Mirror-Neuron System," *Annual Review of Neuroscience* 27 (2004): 169–192, doi:10.1146/annurev.neuro.27.070203.144230.

6 Alliance Feedback

What Seasoned CEOs Know about Helping Others Change

For several years in college, I washed dishes at a cafeteria on the edge of our campus. Most of the employees were students, and the head guy, Mr. Benson, ran the place without a hitch. Mr. Benson, noted for being laid back, created a very pleasant lunch getaway for the university's students, faculty, and staff.

After eating, everyone left their trays at a pass-through window, and I scraped the leftover food into some buckets. We then placed the dishes into a large commercial grade dishwasher. Every day, two farmers who were brothers, Joe and Sam, came by around 2:00 P.M. to pick up the buckets, which were full of a not so appetizing looking mixture of food I had emptied into the buckets over the course of several hours. The farmers used the buckets to *slop their hogs*. I sometimes today use the phrase *a pig's breakfast* to describe a messy problem, and I know of what I speak.

My job was not intellectually stimulating, so some of the other workers and I bantered with each other to pass the time. Being a clever college student, I hadn't quite mastered the social grace to pay attention to other's feelings when joking about something. Every Wednesday, the cafeteria served ham as the entrée. I scrapped ample portions of the baked ham into the slop buckets. That day was particularly

boring, so I decided to tease the farmers. When they came in,
I acted very concerned and said, "Guys, I've been thinking about what
we're feeding the pigs today. Do you realize we are turning them into
cannibals? I mean, think about it. We're feeding them their brethren.
They could be eating their best friend from several months ago."
With every sentence, you could tell that they were more unsettled.
"This just isn't right. These poor animals are violating their conscience
and don't even know they have one. We have to take a stand against
rampant cannibalism here in our own town." My university friends
were laughing, but the farmers were not.

The farmers smiled politely, but it became increasingly obvious
that my glib humor made them very uncomfortable. They gathered
up their buckets and headed out the back door to their truck. Unbe-
knownst to me, Joe and Sam ran into Mr. Benson in the parking lot
and described what had just happened in the dishwashing area. They
were extremely grateful to have free food for their hogs and didn't want
to offend anyone.

Mr. Benson requested I stop by his office after work that afternoon.
He closed the door and asked me to take a seat. "Tim, we love the mission of our cafeteria—to provide healthy, appetizing, and affordable
meals in a pleasant atmosphere for students, faculty, and staff of the
university. We're blessed with a fantastic location and a great team,
including you. A critical part of our team is our group of local farmers.
Some bring us fresh produce and others like Joe and Sam perform a
valuable service by removing hundreds of pounds of food waste from
the cafeteria and putting it to good use. We like how this fits with our
strong environmental stewardship values. Joe and Sam are good men
who love to farm. They are loyal, conscientious, and show up every
day to do their job. They thought you were serious and didn't want to
violate your moral sensibilities. I assured them that they were a critical
part of our team, we valued them and counted on them bringing their
empty buckets to the cafeteria every day. I further told them that they
need not worry at all about offending you in the slightest."

By this point, I slid so low on Mr. Benson's couch he probably lost sight of me. "Tim, as I have come to know you over the last year, I believe you care about people and you care about our cafeteria's mission. I know you're not going to wash dishes the rest of your life, but this is an important time for you to learn to align your actions and words with your values and the values of our cafeteria. I believe that how we treat people matters more than just about anything. I want to support you in expressing who you really are, and so I know you will apologize to Joe and Sam tomorrow afternoon when they stop by to pick up their buckets. Thank you for working here, and I hope you'll remember this as one of the most important jobs you've ever had."

My throat thick with emotion, I could barely utter a word. I assured Mr. Benson that nothing of this sort would ever happen again. I thanked him for talking with me and went out with some humility and wisdom I desperately needed. I came to work the next day not nearly so full of myself and apologized to Joe and Sam. I assured them how much we all appreciated their service to make our cafeteria run smoothly. They laughed and said, "Anyway, pigs can't be cannibals. They can only be *porcusabals*." We became good friends that day.

Mr. Benson did not have an MBA. He was not running a complicated business. He did not get rich from running a simple lunchtime cafeteria in a college town. More importantly, he impacted a lot of people and helped me through a transformational moment. He had every right to whittle me down to nothing and fire me. I had put at risk a key part of his food service process and made fun of some of his dear friends. He chose to help me grow from the experience. I did grow and remember him today as a great boss and role model.

In Chapter 5, we reviewed the compelling evidence that criticism is a very ineffective way to manage people and identified numerous deleterious effects of criticism on our brains. No one who is serious about building a strong workforce (or a healthy family, or winning team, or effective volunteer group) will use criticism or other abusive language to bring people into line.

As I mentioned earlier in the book, I'm not saying these principles apply to everyone in our lives. We cannot attempt to transform everyone with whom we come in contact. There are also any number of occasions realistically when we need to speak with critical directness without concern for bringing out the best in someone. This book addresses how we bring out the best in those we lead, parent, teach, coach, which encompasses a much smaller universe of people!

The understandable question is without the use of negative feedback or criticism, how do we persuade those we lead to change what they are doing when they are off track, being ineffective, making mistakes, or not acting consistently with the mission, goals, or values of the organization? How do we correct someone who's off course without triggering all the problems mentioned in Chapter 5?

Alliance Feedback

Alliance Feedback describes how to get people in line with their own espoused values and aspirations and/or the mission, strategy, goals, and values of their organization. Alliance Feedback *points out contradictions between a person's intentions and his or her present behavior in a supportive manner.*

The word *alliance* conveys the notion that we need to be aligned in this endeavor. Typically, critical feedback is judgmental in that it tells the recipient of the feedback, "You are out-of-line with what I, as your boss, deem to be correct." I am not suggesting that most managers deliver this type of feedback in an unpleasant manner, but I am saying that, unpleasant or not, it places the manager in a clear top-down role of saying, "*You* are/are not meeting *my* expectations." If we want to bring out the best in another person, we are more likely to do so if we form an alliance intended to help the person. Even though I may know a lot more about the job, I'm not your parent. I'm your colleague who is using my judgment and experience to help you excel.

There are two types of Alliance Feedback. The first category is *Aspirational,* which says to the employee, "You have aspirations, hopes, dreams, and personal goals that are important to you, which I want to support you in achieving. Aspire comes from Old French and means "endeavor to obtain, to climb up, or breathe into."[1] Aspirational Feedback tends to be focused on an individual's hopes and dreams. "You are more likely to achieve your aspirations if you do this." Fill in the blank—work with people more collaboratively, approach the problem this way, or listen to the customer more before asserting your agenda. The fundamental idea is to be sure we create a linkage between something the person aspires to achieve and a change he or she needs to make. We are telling the recipient of our contrary perspective to *"Remember your personal why."* The manager is encouraging the subordinate to breathe life into their effort.

The second category of Alliance Feedback is *Missional.* This type of feedback builds upon our mutual or collective desire to accomplish our organization's mission and mutually determined performance goals that we both believe are valuable contributions to the overall enterprise. Feedback of this nature creates a *Missional Alliance.* When an employee departs from actions that support the mission and goals, it provides an opportunity to point out these incongruities.

If we want to bring out the best in another person, we are more likely to do so if we form an alliance intended to help the person.

Missional Feedback includes a manager's and subordinate's joint review of what they set out to accomplish, a review of the progress in reaching our mutually agreed upon goals and how the employee can improve in the months ahead. The most important feature of the Missional Feedback conversation between a boss and subordinate is the establishment of a connection between the employee's work and the mission and goals *which they mutually agree are relevant and important.*

There are eight conditions that make the above approach effective. These perspectives will galvanize our perspective and lay the groundwork for effective Alliance Feedback:

1. Remember that our amygdala possesses an ever-present negativity bias. It's wired to detect threats. In war zones, enemy combatants sometimes lay out *trip wires* with transparent fishing line connected to the detonator of an explosive charge. When we want to help someone grow, we avoid their trip wires and are intentional about making the conversation feel safe. I learned early on in our marriage that it was really stupid for me to tell my wife, Anne, that she was acting like one of her grandmothers. Mamie, bless her heart, was a bit judgmental, critical, and persnickety—other than these qualities, she was a perfectly delightful person! Introducing a comparison to Mamie created a direct route to Anne's amygdala, a surefire method to make the conversation go badly!

2. Another critical aspect of making Alliance Feedback helpful to the recipient is to be sure that we stay grounded ourselves. We need to set aside distractions and make sure the recipient knows that he or she is our only focus at that moment. We need to prepare for the conversation and to make sure the timing is right for both of us. A certain way to activate the amygdala is to convey irritation or impatience, even if it has nothing to do with the person with whom you're meeting.

> *Alliance Feedback raises contradictions* contradictions to a person's present behavior *in a supportive environment.*

Participating in the transformation of another person is costly. One CEO told me, "You have to spend time on how to make this helpful. You don't just go in and blow up the bridge." We pay a significant price to ready ourselves emotionally to deliver Alliance Feedback effectively. I may feel like saying, "When are you going to get your act together?" But the expression of this attitude will doom the efficacy of any feedback I provide. One CEO said, "You have to love someone enough to give them feedback." He's right. We must care about someone to exert the effort to give them thoughtful feedback. It costs us to work through how the information we are imparting comes from the heart and is best for the person.

3. A CEO of a very large organization told me that when his favorite boss gave him feedback, it was always about "betterment." I strongly believe that if we know deep down that a person is *for us*, we can hear just about anything they convey to us. One way to avoid engaging the defensive side of a person's amygdala is to make sure the person feels safe.

A CEO told me that if someone is giving feedback because he is down on you, "It's not feedback. It's abuse." I believe there needs to be a tone that feels like, "With the possible exception of your family, there is no one on the planet more for you than I am. I am committed to your success and advancement in our organization." One CEO told me that even when his boss "criticized" him, it didn't feel like criticism. He said it felt like "affirmation." This is how it should work. A supportive environment is the key to delivering effective Alliance Feedback. One CEO in my interview sample said, I tell the recipients, "I believe you can become your best you!" Another CEO told me that his most influential boss always signed his e-mails to him, "IPOU," which stands for, "I'm proud of you." Apparently, he adopted this practice from Mr. Rogers, but the CEO told me he loved getting that type of encouragement. He said that even "simple encouragement" means a lot.

A CEO told me that if someone is giving feedback because he is down on you, "It's not feedback. It's abuse."

4. Attribute positive motives to the recipient of Alliance Feedback. Mr. Benson did this masterfully with me when he described my wayward humor with Joe and Sam. It's almost a universal certainty that *we judge others by their behavior, while we judge ourselves by our intentions* (usually thought to be good and pure). We can't fully know the circumstances of another person's life, and it helps the recipient of Alliance Feedback to know that we believe they care about the values and mission of our organization. Candidly, I have a cynical, judgmental side that gets in my way sometimes. I must be highly intentional to attribute positive motives. This is especially difficult in highly politicized environments where I know people are trying to advantage themselves in the pecking order. They may, in fact, not have positive motives. I don't think we should be naive about other's motives, but when we start out with a positive attribution of their motives, the likelihood increases that we can truly influence the other person. Mr. Benson may have wondered if I was a complete jerk who thought I was somehow superior to these dumb farmers, but he gave me the benefit of the doubt. He fueled the more noble side of my aspirations with his positive assumptions and brought out the best in me.

A friend of mine rode a subway in New York City to get across town, and to pass the time, he settled into that day's *Wall Street Journal*. He was not paying attention to much going on around him, but he couldn't help but notice three very rambunctious elementary age children nosily running around the subway car. As they swung around the chrome bars playing tag, they bumped into other passengers to their growing annoyance. Some of the older riders were especially wary that the children might cause someone to fall and be injured. The man who was apparently their father was not attempting to rein in his children in the slightest. In fact, he looked at the floor oblivious to his children's behavior and the displeasure of the other riders.

My friend is a loving father but also strict when it comes to his children's behavior, especially in public. By his own admission, he can be tough-minded and a bit judgmental at times regarding the lax parenting he sees in public. He decided it was time to speak up.

My friend leaned over to the father who was sitting nearby and tapped him on the knee. "Sir, I don't know if you are aware, but your children are disturbing the other passengers. Don't you think it would be a good idea to have them sit down?" My friend said that the man appeared to emerge from a deep stupor. He looked around completely oblivious to his children's behavior. "I'm so sorry. We just came from my wife's funeral, and I just . . . ." At that point, he began to weep uncontrollably.

The man's raw pain cut my friend to the core with guilt and remorse for judging so harshly this poor father who grieved his wife's death and realized with far greater finality he must now raise and support three young children alone. My friend felt terrible realizing how quickly he attributed the worst of motives to the father without knowing anything about his life's circumstances.

It is most important to clarify that I am not saying people in our organizations (or our children or our students) should not be responsible for their actions and the outcomes they are charged to achieve. If we categorically know that someone doesn't care about the organization or their work, he or she should be helped to leave (more on this in Chapter 7). Attributing positive motives lifts the plane of the conversation and places the focus on what and how the person can change to be successful. It takes the murky topic of attitude off the table and asks, "How can we help you identify and solve any knowledge or skill deficits or work process glitches?" When we analyze a problem, it dramatically helps the person to assume that he or she wants to be successful.

5. A critical aspect of Aspirational Feedback is that we want to help those we lead to become more self-aware about how *their actions*

that potentially create a barrier to *their aspirations*. One CEO said we want our feedback to " ... cause a person to think deeply about themselves. I want the person to self-reflect and become more self-aware." When giving Alliance Feedback, we must point out any inconsistency of their behavior with their own personal hopes and dreams. Without question, the most powerful motivator for change is what is important to us. We can stress the importance of selfless actions and team first, but we would be shortsighted to not acknowledge that our brains are wired for self-interest.

> *When giving Aspirational Feedback, we must point out any inconsistency of their behavior with their own personal hopes and dreams.*

The following example demonstrates how a corporate leader might tie Alliance Feedback to personal aspirations. "I know you really want to become a vice president and run this department in the next five years. To reach that goal it is essential that you learn to collaborate more effectively and gain support for your initiatives from your peers in other functional areas."

I worked with a highly successful company that discouraged employees from talking about their career aspirations, the assumption being that it was the boss's role to recognize a person's talent and to guide the employee's career progression. It was also thought to restrain any tendency for an employee to self-aggrandize. While I believe the boss does play a critical role in guiding and promoting the development of those he or she leads, it is simply more effective to connect feedback to a compelling personal reason, such as their hopes for progression. Brain science argues for engaging a person's intrinsic motivation, and the benefits of this approach are amazing.

6. Some of the CEOs I interviewed stressed that feedback should be encouraging and challenging at the same time. One told me his favorite boss "put him through the wringer," but with a very clearly

identified motive to make him stronger. He quoted Jesse Owens, the four-time Olympic gold medalist, who said, "If it doesn't challenge you, it won't change you." This CEO added, "Any feedback I offer must have a clear and unmistakable benefit to the person."

Ideally, a boss pairs Alliance Feedback with affirmation, because it makes the feedback even more self-relevant. We are less likely to trivialize or disengage from the Alliance Feedback if paired with affirmation. It also makes a person more resilient to any criticism received from other sources, like disgruntled peers.

7. The tone of the Alliance Feedback conversation must be professional and adult at all times. I occasionally observe leaders give critical feedback that feels like a child being scolded. The "parental manager" talks to employees like children. I recommend a direct tone but not one that seems paternal or maternal.

   One CEO pointed out that his favorite boss early in his career always treated everyone with dignity. Another said when his boss gave him feedback, it never felt "top down." It was always "collaborative and inclusive." Another CEO I interviewed said, "The way I get ready to give someone feedback is to remember that everyone is imperfect, including me!" These perspectives set a healthy tone that we are all trying to grow. They send the message, "I'm not better than you but I've been around the track a few more times. Part of my role is to help you achieve your full potential and not get off track along the way."

8. A CEO said, "Make problems the issue, not the person's character." There is a huge difference between discussing an action versus criticizing a person. Alliance Feedback should be helpful, without being demeaning. Most importantly, it is providing information (for example, a coach telling a player *how* to improve a play) while conveying complete respect for the person. One of the CEOs I interviewed for this book said, "Personal criticism does not have a place in the workplace." Another CEO I interviewed recommended that before providing feedback to a subordinate that

we reflect on our present *attitudinal posture.* "Do I have a "critical spirit' toward this person or am I genuinely trying to help the person?"

Brain research confirms that tying Alliance Feedback to people's hopes, dreams, and aspirations includes the following four benefits:

1. Activates areas of the brain associated with positive emotions, calmness, and an openness to new ideas.[2]

2. Activates brain circuits that are affected by the release of hormones like oxytocin, known for its role in trust and attachment.[3]

3. Activates brain circuits that are associated with the parasympathetic nervous system, which is known to support immune health, cardiovascular health, and hormone balance.[4]

4. Fosters openness to new ideas. In contrast, pointing out people's individual weaknesses activates parts of the brain associated with a stress response.[5]

Caveat Emptor: This Approach May Not Work

One CEO summed up her perspective on feedback by saying, "The key to delivering feedback that a subordinate might view as critical is to have a foundation of trust and relationship." *I am not naïve to the reality that some who make it into a senior management role, including the highest levels, are not trustworthy or necessarily even care about a relationship with their subordinates.* I have actually seen some senior leaders *weaponize* their feedback. I've met many senior executives who I did not believe to be honest and well intentioned enough to apply these principles with integrity and consistency. As discussed in Chapter 4, to bring out the best in another person, we must have an intact core ourselves. Absent that, the principles espoused in this book become irrelevant.

To those who have a boss lacking an intact core, I extend my deepest sympathy. Some people's personal circumstances do not permit changing jobs, or the size of the company may limit your internal mobility. I do urge you to aggressively look for other options. Sometimes, finding an advocate in HR makes sense. The riskiest moves are to confront the person or to go to his or her boss with your concerns. Seek the counsel of a trusted advisor about your best options.

Even if we fully buy into the philosophy and practices of this book, there are people in our organizations who will not benefit from or receive Alliance Feedback, even when well intentioned and skillfully delivered. When we are in a position to recognize that a person for whom we have management responsibility is not responding to our most altruistic attributions and transparent desire to bring out the best in them, what do we do? This is the subject of the next chapter.

Notes

1. https://www.etymonline.com/word/aspire

2. G. L. Cohen, J. Aronson, and C. M. Steele, "When Beliefs Yield to Evidence: Reducing Biased Evaluation by Affirming the Self," *Personality and Social Psychology Bulletin* 26, no. 9 (2000): 1151–1164, doi:10.1177/01461672002611011.

3. C. K. W. De Dreu, "Oxytocin Modulates Cooperation within and Competition between Groups: An Integrative Review and Research Agenda," *Hormones and Behavior* 61, no. 3 (2012): 419–428, http://dx.doi.org/10.1016/j.yhbeh.2011.12.009.

4. R. E. Boyatzis, M. L. Smith, and N. Blame, "Developing Sustainable Leaders through Coaching and Compassion," *Academy of Management Learning & Education* 5, no. 1 (2006): 8–24.

5. G. L. Cohen et al., "When Beliefs Yield to Evidence."

7 Extraordinary Influence for Underperformers

Bringing Out the Best in Someone Who Has Lost His Way

The fundamental premise of *Extraordinary Influence* rests on the belief that bringing out the best in others embodies a leader's highest calling. Affirmation of someone's *customary style* and *competence* contribute significantly to that aim. Speaking Words of Life into a person's *core* can be truly transformational.

Another basic premise of this book—Alliance Feedback (connecting a needed change to a person's personal aspirations) provides a powerful means to bring someone into alignment with the goals, mission, strategies, and culture of the organization.

Performance problems are usually addressed individually. Though not always, performance problems are typically rooted in a person's ineffective style, their lack of competence, or a breached core or some combination of the three.

Some critically important questions:

- How do we bring out the best in others experiencing performance problems?
- Are there instances in which a person and his or her work performance problems simply cannot be remedied?
- If we embark on an effort to develop a person, what are the chances of success?
- Can we realistically bring out the best in anyone?

Performance problems are typically rooted in a person's ineffective style, their lack of competence, or a breached core or some combination of the three.

To answer these questions, let's consider three true stories.

True Story 1

When I finished graduate school and started my first consulting company, Anne gave me a beautiful antique desk with a hand-tooled, tan-colored leather top. The desk was a work of art and became a prized possession. It remains the centerpiece of my personal office.

A new administrator in our firm made some significant mistakes on some work I requested she complete. To make amends, one morning she stopped by the muffin shop in our office building and bought my favorite—a blueberry muffin with the great crispy top. She delivered it to my office before I arrived that morning and set the delicious muffin right on my leather-topped desk with no plate, no napkin—nothing between my desk and the waxed paper muffin wrapper. When I arrived, my eyes went immediately to a giant oily splotch underneath the muffin on my beautiful desk top. The cooking oil from the muffin had wicked straight into the leather leaving an ugly dark blob. When some of the other team members realized what had happened, they sprang into action to try to get the oil out of the leather but to no avail. They even quoted Shakespeare, "Out, out damned spot." Our newest staff member quietly withdrew to the materials production room.

Melissa was very principled, highly intelligent, and interpersonally skilled, but she didn't have the skill set or personality to do the growing load of demanding and detailed administrative work in our office. The muffin blob was not the real problem, but it served as the catalyst we needed to address her challenges at the office.

We were at a moment of truth, not because of my desk, but because of the poor fit between her strengths and the requirements of the job. In the process of talking with a few trusted staff members, some important information surfaced. Melissa hated detailed administrative work. Her passion was interior design, and she desperately wanted to find a way to enter that business. We decided it best that she move on but with a transition period that helped her pursue her higher aspirations.

Melissa seemed quite relieved and appreciative that we gave her a long runway to transition into a new job. Three months later, she left the firm to apprentice under a leading interior designer in town. Melissa's performance problems also reminded us that if we want to hire an excellent person for a particular job, there is no substitution for a discipline process that vets the person in every way possible to ensure a good fit. We performed this service for our clients, but the "cobbler's children had no shoes." Over the years, Melissa's oily muffin spot on my desk faded into other accidents, including my own coffee spills. Those accidents created a nice patina, thus adding beauty to the desk!

Did Melissa have a flawed core? Not in the slightest. She simply didn't have the style and competence to excel in an administrative position. I was at fault for not being more careful to learn about her lack of administrative skill and interest in advance of hiring her. Should we have attempted to develop her skills for the position? Her interests lay elsewhere, and we had no conviction that a developmental effort would be successful.

True Story 2

The CEO of an organization in the hospitality industry contacted me and expressed frustration about an executive in his company who performed quite well in his job, but the five other members of the executive team did not trust him. The CEO said, "David could be the person with the highest potential to succeed me but not if he can't get the rest of the team behind him. The CEO asked, "Can you fix him?" Several weeks later, I flew to Chicago to meet with the "fixee" and the other members of the executive team.

The problems that consistently surfaced in my interviews were that David:

- Talked too much and didn't listen to his other team members.
- Had a terminal case of certainty on any topic, even when there was no basis.
- Didn't show respect for the opinions of others.
- Sometimes walked too close to the edge on spending limits and other corporate policies when entertaining prospects.
- Had to be the star attraction for any event involving clients or prospects.
- Did not develop others in his areas of responsibility.
- Exercised careless management of his own direct reports.

Universal appreciation for David's capabilities equaled his peers' uneasiness about his limitations. Everyone hoped he could change, while expressing strong beliefs that it was unlikely to happen given the depth of his problems. David and I agreed to work together with a focus on helping him further develop his leadership potential and address the concerns of his boss and peers.

David and I decided that he would complete a multirater feedback instrument (sometimes called 360 Feedback) and a couple of other psychological assessments. A good multirater instrument provides very detailed and candid behavioral insight into how others see the person being rated. The results of David's 360 were dreadful and provided quite a blow to his ego—the findings clearly stood in stark contrast to his self-perceptions. We spent the next several meetings reviewing the findings and talking about what types of changes were needed.

Pain sometimes provides an effective source of motivation to grow. Joined with the prospect of a bigger job in the future, David worked extremely hard on the areas of improvement that we agreed were the highest priorities. Over the course of the next 18 months, this individual took the reins of his own development and made remarkable progress. Every month, I received some type of communication acknowledging David's progress. He forged dramatically better relationships with his executive peers. He showed respect, listened to their views, and collaborated on many cross-functional problems. Team morale improved, and his peers became his biggest advocates. Everyone considered him to be an excellent candidate for the top job in a few more years.

True Story 3

A friend's electronics components company grew rapidly and became much more operationally complex. He hired a new vice president of operations to address a myriad of problems. Phillip appeared to have exactly the right kind of background and joined my friend's company with great expectations that he could bring calm to the storm.

Keeping up with customer demands stretched everyone to the limit. Phillip and others worked long hours attempting to improve their shipping time while adding additional SKUs to their product offerings. Their inventory ballooned, tying up cash. The business line of credit nearly maxed out, and some quality problems emerged in some of their legacy products. Everyone reached a 10 on the stress meter.

Phillip displayed some dark and previously undetected aspects of his personality about a year after joining the company. He pried into people's personal lives and insisted he know the specific reasons why they couldn't work overtime on some weekends. He fermented dissent among some of the company's other managers. A hallmark of my friend's company was that he paid his staff well and ensured that the working conditions were excellent. Phillip criticized the CEO and said their compensation was too low. Phillip's arrogantly displayed disrespect for the CEO and the company culture infuriated many of the company's most loyal employees.

Others described Phillip as "mean spirited." He made comments to female employees that were unwelcome and offensive. Complaints about Phillip increased. My friend met with him to discuss the complaints. Phillip exploded with anger and insisted that if not for him, the firm would be falling apart. The intensity of Phillip's vitriol and the disrespect he displayed shocked my friend.

Firm morale declined and teamwork weakened. My friend attempted to coach Phillip but finally gave him a written warning that his behavior must change to keep his job. Phillip did not change, and my friend fired him a few weeks later.

I did not know Phillip well, but the few times he and I talked, I sensed some troubling problems under the surface of his personality. He initially managed to keep his problems contained, but the stress of the rapidly growing business outpaced his ability to rein in his considerable flaws.

Was there something fundamentally wrong with Phillip? Yes. I could only speculate about the origin of his problems, but when my friend asked my advice, I said that no amount of coaching would provide an adequate remedy. I told him, "You need to get him out before he does more damage."

The Three Stories Called for Three Different Remedies

1. Melissa was a *person with a problem* that could not be remedied with feedback and coaching. She was a gifted person in the wrong job. She needed encouragement to pursue her dream. We affirmed her honesty about her aspirations but also agreed that her lack of competence for the work we needed accomplished in our firm was a bridge too far.

2. David was a *person with a problem*, who needed intensive professional coaching. His exceptional job performance and receptivity to change proved his great value to the organization. He needed someone to provide Alliance Feedback in a supportive environment for him to make some fundamental changes.

3. Phillip was a *problem person*. It required significant stress and time for his darker side to emerge, but his core was breached. His negative impact on the organization far exceeded any value he might bring. *For the sake of the greater good*, he needed to leave the company.

Performance problems emerge for a host of reasons after someone works in an organization. We know people who were promoted beyond their competence. We know people whose life circumstances changed and began to impose upon the person's performance at work. We know people whose stress tolerance proved to be inadequate for the demands of a position.

We are always who we are given enough time and enough stress.

Savvy leaders size up whether *the person has a problem* or *he/she is a problem person*. Discerning this difference becomes one of the most worrisome problems we face as leaders. In my first example, Melissa was a person with a problem. David, in the second example, was a person with a problem, but it required some time and developmental resources to determine whether he could change. Phillip, in the third example, was a problem person, for whom no reasonable amount of development would change the fundamental trajectory of his breeched core. Melissa and Phillip left their respective organizations, but for very different reasons. Melissa demonstrated great skill when working out of her strengths. Phillip manifested some serious problems in his core, which were missed in the vetting stage. One problem we all experience in vetting the talent and condition of someone's core is that a person's real self surfaces only with time and stress. We are always who we are given enough time and enough stress.

The major idea of this chapter holds that we must be good stewards of our organization's resources (time, energy, and often, money). We must be able to quickly size up whether we should deploy resources to get a person in line with the mission, strategies, goals, and culture of the company.

The problem is that culture by its very nature can be fragile. My grandmother liked to say, "One bad apple spoils the barrel." Food experts affirm this truth in pointing out that a rotten apple releases chemicals that rot the neighboring apples. A problem person, especially in a leadership role, can precipitate a major decay in the huge asset of strong culture and values. In my example, I predicted that if Phillip stayed in my friend's company much longer, it would have taken years to build back the good will my friend labored so hard to construct.

Members of an organization expect their leaders to make these hard determinations and follow with action. Our own credibility sometimes suffers irreparable damage when we don't act decisively to address problem people. Strong individuals often leave the organization when leaders refuse to act in these matters over time.

How Do We Make These Judgments That Have Such a Huge Impact on People's Lives?

When a person works in our organization and exhibits poor performance, how do we make the distinction between a person with a problem and a problem person? I often ask myself or the leader a series of questions, which I find helpful in getting to the right answer quickly.

1. Is the person performing their job overall with excellence? "Yes" or "No."

2. How well do the person's skills, ability, and temperament fit the requirements of the position? *Great Fit/Adequate Fit/Poor Fit.*

3. Does the person's poor performance seem to be temporary, circumstantial, or more enduring? For example, does the person need to acquire technical knowledge or other skills to perform well in their job? Are there circumstances that account for an individual's temporary drop in performance, such as an ailing parent who needs special attention? Does the person work under a perpetual cloud of tension or constantly seem out of synch with the team?

4. What is the likelihood that the person in question can perform well in their job in the future within a reasonable time frame? *High Likelihood/Low Likelihood.*

In answering the fourth question, it behooves us to be brutally honest. In Melissa's case, we could have structured her job differently, but the improvised role would not accomplish what our firm definitively needed. She really longed to find a job more suited to her skills, temperament, and interests. In Phillip's case, my friend gave him feedback on many occasions without appreciable improvement.

Phillip's problems were too deep-seated with no reasonable prospect that he could make the necessary changes. He had to go.

To Whom Should We Direct Our Limited Developmental Resources?

What are the risks and rewards of helping someone with performance problems? The following table offers a way of evaluating the likelihood of success:

Type of Problem	Example from the Three Stories	Likelihood of Success	Action Needed
Style	David (Person with a Problem)	Excellent to Good if Coachable	Alliance Feedback Coaching/ Mentoring
Competence	Melissa (Person with a Problem)	Good to Modest	Developmental Training if person has aptitude and interest.
Core	Phillip (Problem Person)	Poor	Leave the Organization

I pointed out earlier that leaders potentially exert extraordinary influence on followers and help bring out their best capabilities. A major dilemma is that we cannot exert extraordinary influence over everyone. Some individuals struggle within themselves such that no amount of affirmation or Alliance Feedback or other developmental resources can bring them in line *inside the boundaries of our organization.* Any number of resources may help heal a person's core, but any job with even normal day-to-day stresses is not the best place to get well, especially when their problems impose themselves on others. No one is perfect, and we all have a shadow in our core. We must have compassion for all, while also recognizing that even healthy organizations are fragile. Compassion must be married to judgment and courage when dealing with a problem person.

A major dilemma is that we cannot exert extraordinary influence over everyone.

How Much Compassion?

It's not always easy to help a problem person leave the organization. Leaders express to me upon occasion that they believe that poorly performing individuals deserve the right to grow, and that under the right circumstances they will rise like the mythical Phoenix to leadership greatness. The question we must pose is, *at what expense?* A problem person often wreaks havoc on an organization. The amount of energy needed to address the internal disruptions caused by a problem person are often stunning. Some organizations spend so much time and emotional energy trying to achieve internal harmony, it seriously compromises their ability to achieve external goals and make a profit. A client organization almost lost their most gifted player recently, because they would not deal with a problem person. The emotional pain this problem person caused over a long period of time merited his firing years earlier.

Some organizations spend so much time and emotional energy trying to achieve internal harmony, it seriously compromises their ability to achieve external goals and make a profit.

I know that some readers will take issue with my opinions expressed in the last few paragraphs. They advocate that with proper coaching and encouragement, even a person with a problem can overcome their difficulties. Other readers who have a strong personal religious faith maintain that any person can be redeemed and transformed. While I agree with those views in theory, I believe that most organizations pursue a different mission than the personal healing of some excruciatingly disruptive traits or wayward actions in their employees.

This may appear to conflict with this book's theme of bringing out the best in others, but the pain inflicted upon those who must work closely with the problem person, the disruption to teams, and the diminishment of cultural health caused by fundamentally unhealthy individuals supersedes the developmental needs of a given individual. I argue that helping problem people leave the organization is, in fact, a key element to bringing out the best in others. The impact of a problem person can be so toxic if not removed that a leader forfeits the opportunity to bring out the best in those needed to conduct the vital work of the organization.

Leaders are stewards of organizational health and to not remove highly disruptive people, even if the problem person achieves results valuable to the organization, is very shortsighted. To force a person's dark tensions and instabilities on others trying to do their jobs conscientiously may appear noble to some, but in actuality, it eviscerates the hope and joy of the work for so many others affected by the problem person. I also wonder if, in some cases, a leader's stated compassion is, in fact, a cover for lack of courage to address the problem directly.

Resistance to Dealing with a Problem Person

We may encounter considerable headwinds when attempting to remove a problem person from the organization. The person may possess certain attributes deemed vital. Perhaps key technical skills, industry knowledge, or vital sales relationships appear to be irreplaceable.

In making the case for terminating a problem person, the leader should first demonstrate that he is acutely aware of the value the problem person brings to the organization and the risks of firing him or her. The leader ideally demonstrates some sense of calibration for the fallout from the firing and some plan to mitigate the risk. These steps lay the groundwork for change. The CEO should encourage any detractors to express their views in the proper setting, but then seek consensus on the needed action.

Every person serving in an organization has a *value/price index*. This sounds harsh, so let me point out that I do not mean this existentially or spiritually, but rather in the sense of the value of a person's contribution to the organization and the corresponding price of their involvement. Financial compensation is certainly a consideration but more importantly, some people are very high maintenance (and I don't mean what the person orders for lunch). A problem person often requires a lot of damage control from their actions with others. A CEO who wants to fire a problem person must make a compelling case for how that individual's price exceeds his or her considerable value to the organization.

One approach I've seen used effectively is for the person advocating the departure of a problem person to use a powerful example of damage caused to others. I know of one organization in the Midwest where the CEO disclosed that the most successful vice president of sales in the company's history was considering a job offer from a competitor because he simply could not work one more day with a very toxic vice president of marketing. Everyone knew the head of marketing was a problem, but she brought so much value to the company through social media and other nontraditional channels. Some members of the executive team deemed *her* to be irreplaceable. When the CEO dropped the bombshell that the VP of sales might leave because of her, it changed the calculus on the VP of marketing's value/price index.

The senior team went into a frenzy figuring out how to reel back in the VP of sales, including parting ways with the VP of marketing.

The Him or Me Card

The ultimate escalation in dealing with a problem person is the *him or me card*. Sometimes opposition to a problem person's departure is intense. The CEO and a few others might feel strongly that a person needs to leave, but others may believe his or her unique value makes that person essential to the future of the company. The him or me card realistically can only be played once in the tenure of most leaders. A CEO of a Florida construction company played this card in a meeting with a group of senior managers in order to fire a very popular (but disloyal) member of the team. It took the opposition's knees out. The problem person was gone within a couple of days; however, the cost to the CEO's standing with the members of the opposition was incredibly high. The CEO will be rebuilding trust for a long time with those leaders who opposed his decision. It was a very heavy-handed move, but the CEO felt the problem person to be so disruptive that he had to go.

Ideally, a strong consensus emerges around helping a problem person to depart the organization, such that no one actively opposes the move. When leaders skillfully manage the departure of a problem person, it often provides tremendous relief. I firmly believe that decisions at the top are more about building alignment among diverse constituencies. Alignment needs to be built so that a critical mass of those impacted most by a decision are on board. When a senior leader determines that a problem person needs to move on, it's really about timing—securing agreement among the right stakeholders.

The Virtue of Redemption

The narrative that is implanted into the collective psyche of an organization when a person with a problem changes, grows, and realizes their potential is of paramount value to the health of any organization's culture, as in the case of David. By the way, he has become a serious CEO succession candidate. Redemptive stories are truly uplifting.

We will now turn our focus to special applications of extraordinary influence. The attention up to now considered the application of these principles to an individual. What is the relevance to teams—the topic of the next chapter.

Part III
Special Applications of Extraordinary Influence

8 Extraordinary Influence for Teams

Three Levers for High Performance

One of my closest friends worked his way through college on a commercial landscape crew. One day "Pat" and the other team members installed some large aesthetic boulders on the edge of a freshly paved sidewalk, which traversed a beautiful nature park. A few members of the team, including my friend, were trained in using a bucket crane to lift the boulders and position them in the location specified in the landscape plan.

The only control in the cab for which Pat did not know the purpose was a red lever on the right side of the control panel. To this day, Pat does not know what got into him, but he impulsively reached over and pulled the red lever. Instantly, the jaws of the giant bucket swung open dropping a several ton boulder from about 10 feet into the middle of a freshly paved asphalt sidewalk. To describe it as a disaster far understates the destruction. It looked like a giant meteor crashed on the lunar surface. The team spent the rest of the day and much of the next getting the boulder out the crater and repairing the damage.

Despite being a strong contributor to the team and well-liked by all, Pat knew he would be fired for this costly mistake. As a result, he would have to drop out of school. His dreams for his future were crushed. The rest of his life would be spent asking the same question hundreds of times a day, "Do you want fries with that?" As he stood in line to get his paycheck on Friday afternoon, he girded himself for the worst. His boss handed Pat what he knew to be his last paycheck.

Pat's boss could have said, "You screwed up and cost the company a lot of money in unnecessary labor, so you're fired." Instead, his message included a surprising affirmation. "Your mistake yesterday was highly uncharacteristic of you. You are an excellent employee, and we greatly value your membership on our installation team and the positive influence you have on the other team members. We want you to remain on the team, and by the way, don't pull that red lever again unless you know exactly why you're doing it!" The boss spoke Words of Life to Pat's core.

When Pat's team assembled for their beginning of day check in at the office on Monday morning, everyone wanted to know what the boss said on Friday afternoon. Pat told the story, and everyone became quiet. Normally, the meeting was all banter replaying the weekend games, but something was different. Pat kept his job, which everyone felt good about, but the grace shown to Pat enveloped the whole team. Everyone knew Pat should have been fired, but forgiving his mistake affirmed the whole team and created a much broader impact than just one person. When Pat pulled the red lever, all reaped the consequences, but all benefitted from the grace shown to one in the supervisor's Words of Life.

The mission of Pat's landscaping company was, "We create beautiful spaces that renew people's lives and preserve the environment." That day, even the mission took on more meaning. Though they faced another day of hard physical labor, the team experienced the goodness of their corporate purpose. The team's commitment to the mission rose through the affirmation of one team member.

The Three Levers

A constant interplay exists among three dimensions in our lives—the *I*, the *We*, and the *It*.[1] The *I* represents our individual hopes, dreams, and concerns. The *We* represents the collective aspirations, interests, and potential conflicts among the group members. The *It* expresses our purpose, mission, task, or quest.

A lever can be thought of as *a great effect from a small cause*. Pat pulled a physical lever in the crane, which allowed a small hand motion to move a huge boulder. For a leader, these three dimensions function as levers. A leader's attention to the individuals, the group, and the task constitute levers a leader uses to manage a team or even a whole organization.

Balanced attention to the I, the We, and the It is absolutely necessary for a healthy leadership team, a well-functioning military unit, and even a family. When any dimension remains out-of-balance, all three dimensions suffer in some way. Much of this book addresses what a leader must do to transform an individual, the *I*. A group or team encompasses the *I*, the *We*, and the *It*. In the normal course of work, teams oscillate. For a team to perform with excellence, all three

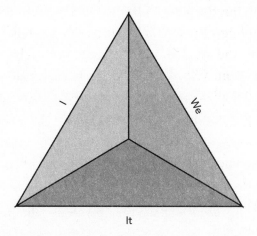

Figure 8.1 Balancing of the "I, We and It."

require balanced attention. When any of the three is over or under emphasized, problems ensue. Despite the constantly shifting needs of a normal team, a skilled leader must learn to lever all three dimensions to restore the team to balance.

One of the most dysfunctional executive teams with which I've ever worked led a manufacturing company in the central United States. The team included one of the most disruptive members I've ever seen hold a job in the corporate world. People literally speculated that he must hold incriminating information on a senior officer in the company who protected him. Other team members were quite talented in their respective functions and had important ideas to grow the company, but the one individual constantly drew disproportionate attention to himself. He could take the whole team into the abyss of despair faster than imaginable. He perfectly fit what the great southern author, Joel Chandler Harris, called a "tar baby." It was impossible to have a clean, congruent, unencumbered, straightforward conversation with the team's tar baby without getting stuck. Many meetings ended with members shaking their heads in disbelief, wondering how in the world the guy kept his job. The excessive focus on the one highly dysfunctional individual made it impossible to experience the synergy of the collective *We* or team, and the accomplishment of the mission suffered appalling compromise. He was what my grandmother would call a *mess*.

In this example, an inordinate amount of attention was focused on the one dysfunctional member. He absorbed a dramatically excessive amount of energy and time from the leader and the members of the team. As a result of one highly dysfunctional member, the team became dysfunctional, because the team leader did not act quickly or with adequate resolve to address the problem.

The three dimensions of team member, team, and mission are highly interdependent, and when not in relative balance, the team loses its stability. It's like a three-legged stool with only one or two legs. Working as a team usually proves much more difficult than anyone appreciates, especially when one or more members carry some emotional baggage as did the dysfunctional individual in the example. The level of rancor and tension I see on many teams often shocks even a grizzled veteran like me.

Great leaders know how to bring out the best in teams through maintaining balance among the individual team members, the collective team, and an inspiring mission. A team leader must keep these aspects in balance to experience the power of teamwork so often touted. At any moment in time, the leader must bring one of these three entities to the forefront through nimble attention to any imbalance. Most underperforming teams lack balance and proper emphasis on one or several of these dimensions. How does this work?

Individual Team Members—the *I*

We might ask, "Why do individual concerns need attention—we're building a team?" A dedicated team focus in some organizations means that attention to the *I* runs totally counter to teamwork, so I would like to challenge this notion.

Reader warning—I am not a big fan of slogans, especially inspirational slogans on posters, and even less, those slogans that are expensively framed behind glass. I should be careful here, because a lot of us have bought those sappy inspirational posters for the workplace walls. These inspirational slogans presumably inspire us to work enthusiastically with others and subjugate our interests to a group of people I sometimes don't even like, much less trust.

A couple of my least favorite slogans are:

"There's no 'I' in Team."

Actually, there *is* an *I* in team. It's the individual team members. I like Bill Murray's tweet about this popular slogan. "There's no 'I' in team … there is, however, an 'I' in win, achievement, prevail, triumph, first place, gold medalist, and champion."[2]

"Things get easy when we work together."

Whoever said "Things get easy when we work together," has never been on a team or tried to work with another person for more than an hour. My observation over the last 30 years of helping hundreds of organizations is that work often becomes incredibly difficult when we work with others.

"Better *we* than *me*."

Most of the team training I've led personally, and most of the team training I've studied seeks primarily to build the collective *We* of the team. Individual team members must also be developed according to their specific needs and acknowledged for their individual contributions. Focus on the *We* to the exclusion of the *I* creates an imbalance team leaders must address.

All my cynicism about well-intended team slogans aside, team leaders must find ways to recognize and to affirm the individual members of a team. Compensation, titles, special recognition, and career paths represent just a few examples of actions that can be considered for individuals on even the most healthy and well-functioning teams. Attention to individuals does not reflect inattention to the team.

Me First?

Attention to an individual team member could mistakenly appear to foster a "me first" attitude or narcissism. Rather, as individuals we exist distinct from others. We have our own hopes, dreams, plans, and aspirations that are important to us. We hold opinions and insights that we self-authored. We have our own voices and our own part of the mission. As Stephen Jobs said, we all want to make our own dent in the universe. Any team leader who ignores the individual needs of team members invites a highly disruptive imposition of those needs on the performance of the team.

Conversely, excessive attention to any individual for any reason, positive or negative, creates an imbalance. Problem individuals such as the one described earlier in this chapter drain energy and passion away from a team to the point of disillusioned team spirit and lack of focus on the accomplishment of the team's task or mission. The *We* and the *It* or team purpose suffer.

When leading a team session, I always try to begin with an exercise that speaks to the needs of all the *Is* for recognition. Asking a question or two that each team member answers about himself/herself gets a meeting rolling. Here are some simple examples:

Where did you grow up?

What did you do after high school?

Give a 60-second summary of your career highlights.

What is an interesting but unknown fact about you?

Who has been the person of greatest influence in your life?

What would you do if you won the lottery?

What do you hope to get from this team session?

A warm-up exercise, such as these sample questions, engages the I and creates a readiness to attend to the *We* and the *It*. One other important practice for *I* behavior in a team setting is to explain any unusual behavior. I sometimes point out to groups, "Distractions take precedence." If an individual member leaves the meeting, for example, everyone wonders if something is wrong.

One team member, in a session I led, announced at the beginning of the meeting that his wife may be starting labor. "She had false contractions two days ago, but this may be the real thing. She will text me, so if I leave suddenly, you'll know why." Five minutes later, he darted from the room. We understood the sudden departure and wished the first-time parents well! His announcement of his possible departure from the meeting honored the *We*, and legitimized the *I*'s uncharacteristic behavior.

Extraordinary Influence on the *We*

To harvest the benefits of teamwork, an effective team leader must generate a strong sense of the *We*. Like any enduring relationship, the potential synergy of working with others does not spontaneously materialize. It requires disciplined intentionality. Extraordinary influence on a team requires that the leader equip the team with the necessary skills and processes to be a great *We*. Many excellent books have been written on the topic of how to build an effective team, such as MacMillan's *The Performance Factor* and Lencioni's *The Five Dysfunctions of a Team*.

> *Like any enduring relationship, the potential synergy of working with others does not spontaneously materialize. It requires disciplined intentionality.*

Just as with individuals, leaders must provide both tactical and strategic affirmation to the team. Oddly, I rarely see team leaders affirm teams for doing something extraordinary together. Well-documented performance gains often result from a highly functioning team, such as greater productivity and a higher quality work product. These are the domain of tactical influence.

Although we normally think of "core" as an individual attribute, as discussed in earlier chapters, the *We* also has a collective core, which reflects the team's character! Teams also adopt collective beliefs that guide team behavior.

A Team's Collective Core

I often observe a self-concept in teams, which effectively reveals the health of the team's *collective core*. Some teams are confident, inter-dependent, and collaborative across their respective functional areas. They have a pride about their team's work and believe in the power of their well-functioning *We*. They trust each other to do their jobs and they trust in each other's integrity. While they may have conflict periodically, the disagreements lead to clarity versus rancor.

I observe other teams with a terrible self-concept. They exhibit very low trust in each other. The team stays mired in conflict with minimal progress on important initiatives. During meetings, members constantly check their phones. There is eye-rolling and sighing when certain members speak. Their attendance at meetings is obligatory, and members are grateful when the meeting is short. The team is toxic.

Words of Life (strategic influence) must also be given to affirm the character of a team. The 10 dimensions described in Chapter 4 (Integrity, Courage, Humility, Judgment, Authenticity, Self-regulation, Wisdom, Candor, Resilience, and Influence) also apply to the *We*. How the team accomplished its work, for example, being resilient in the presence of repeated setbacks, is a great way to affirm a team. When a team is healthy and well-functioning, Words of Life should be spoken to the team's core. When a team is dysfunc-tional, Alliance Feedback is in order. As I discussed in Chapter 7, it may be important to help certain members move off the team.

Following are four dimensions that invite affirmation of the *We* with Words of Life when a team performs well.

1. Respect for fellow team members. Every interaction among team members must manifest regard for each other.

2. Openness and candor on the part of all team members. Hidden agendas spell doom for team trust.

3. Participation emotionally and mentally. When team members are physically present but emotionally absent, the spirit of the team evaporates.

4. Empathy for each person on the team. Team members must show appreciation for the inherent reality that each team experiences a constant barrage of distractions, competing interests, and conflict from a variety of sources.

Extraordinary Influence on the *It*—the Mission or Quest of the Team

When thoughtfully formed and skillfully communicated, a purpose or mission (the *It*) provides motivation for the team. A great mission becomes a *quest*. A team leader exerts extraordinary influence with this powerful tool. It contains the potential to take even the most mundane work or project and lifts the collective self-esteem.

A great team mission becomes a quest.

The leading hotelier in the world and founder of the Ritz Carlton Hotel Company and Capella Hotels, Horst Schulze, makes a practice of personally opening all his new hotels. We would probably agree that public perception ranks some hotel jobs lower on the desirability scale, such as housekeepers. Yet, Schulze urges his housekeepers to be the best in the world. During training, he stresses to housekeepers, "We are ladies and gentlemen serving ladies and gentlemen." Along with many other supporting policies and expectations, housekeepers are empowered to make many decisions in the interest of providing a superior customer experience to all guests. Schulze's mission to be the best, supported with hundreds of other quality practices, led to the Ritz Carlton receiving the prestigious Malcomb Baldridge award, not once but twice, thus making it the only company in the hotel industry to achieve such a distinction. Schulze has also trained seven hotel managers presently serving as heads of major hotel chains.

Schulze's mission to be the best might better be described as a *quest*. His quest mobilized an army of dedicated hotel managers, concierges, food service professionals, valets, dishwashers, and housekeepers excited about changing the world of lodging for discriminating guests.

A great mission creates purpose, meaning, passion, and even urgency for a team. Leaders who want to provide extraordinary leadership for teams (and organizations) transform the task into a quest. Connecting a seemingly mundane task to a higher calling raises the importance and even the self-esteem of those completing the task. Putting new tires on a car can be about air wrenches or about keeping a family safe. It's the same task, but one perspective inspires a different level of attention to detail and excellence.

A great mission creates purpose, meaning, passion, and even urgency for a team.

Pressing meaning into the task provides the inspiration and the energy of high-performing teams. If a team lacks passion, find out if they are putting lug nuts on a wheel rim or providing safe travel for families. No matter what the team's task, a great team leader forms and communicates the bigger *why*.

The accomplishment of a great mission provides the leader with tremendous opportunities to affirm the team. *This requires tactical affirmation of the team's style and competence along the way, and strategic affirmation of the team's collective core at key intervals.* Everyone wants to be on a winning team, and accomplishment of a mission becomes the ultimate affirmation.

Extraordinary Influence—Healing the *I*, *We*, and *It* of the Broken Organization or Team

Tragedy or misconduct sometimes occur in any organization. Leaders with whom I've worked died unexpectedly. A chemical plant my firm served experienced a huge explosion, and six people died. Financial misconduct of a leader I knew left a leadership team in denial and disruption.

Sometimes a leader inherits a team or even a whole organization with a trauma or some other besetting concern in its past. A trauma diminishes trust to the extent that even the fundamental economic value of a company is often jeopardized, such as what transpired with Enron.

Eric Pillmore joined Tyco International as senior vice president of corporate governance just after the FBI indicted CEO Dennis Kozlowski for larceny—stealing hundreds of millions of dollars from Tyco (remember the $6,000 shower curtain for his Manhattan apartment?). Pillmore took on the job of restoring the corporate trust with investors, customers, and employees. I spoke with Mr. Pillmore and asked him how he restored that trust. Many thousands of words in articles and other publications as well as video interviews document the details of Tyco's fall and rebirth. My purpose here is to summarize a few of the initiatives Pillmore and his colleagues took to address the immediate needs of *I*, *We*, and *It* on the heels of Kozlowski's fall.

Healing the *I*

Human nature prompts any normal person to prioritize self-interest in a crisis. What will happen to me, my job, my reputation, or my family because of this trauma? This required immediate attention to the *I*. Pillmore said that the leadership team agreed early on that they must act decisively. There was no time for studies and analysis. Two hundred thousand employees and thirty thousand leaders—two hundred and thirty thousand *I*s needed reassurance from senior leadership.

Tyco's senior leaders began the healing process with hundreds of town halls, which "gave the individual employees their voice." Leaders stayed at these sessions for as long as anyone wanted to ask questions. "At first, all people wanted to do was vent. They just wanted to be heard."

As we acknowledged earlier, shame is one of the most powerful and corrosive human emotions. Public shame such as my company's CEO perp walking on TV become private *I* shame. A critical aspect of turning around a wounded team or organization is to restore everyone's pride. At one point, Pillmore knew healing was underway when one questioner joked, "When can I put my Tyco t-shirt back on to mow the lawn?" At the beginning of the town hall initiative, senior leaders were "dogs," but eventually, "We received standing ovations." Town halls and the openness of the leaders who led them opened the door to the reestablishment of trust.

Tyco ran an ad in the *Wall Street Journal*, in which the 13 top leaders pledged, "This month, Tyco is launching an advertising campaign in major newspapers and financial publications in the United States, Europe, and Asia." The ads show Tyco's top 13 executives, their signatures, and a headline that reads, "We signed on because we believe Tyco has a bright future. We signed below to show you we mean it." In essence, the message conveyed that the leaders committed to stay involved in the company until they got it fixed. While the ad's message intended to reassure stockholders and customers, the senior leaders really hoped to assure individual employees. It did.

The creation of a positive emotional bond with the *I*s of a wounded organization or team becomes the focus of restoring trust with the *I*s on a team or a large organization. Visible leadership, non-defensive attention to injured member's apprehensions and a willingness to act in response to employees' concerns must be the hallmarks of this effort.

Healing the *We*

When a breach of trust occurs, no one knows who to trust. Creating a boundary of safety or circle of trust becomes paramount. Tyco's effort to restore trust included a new emphasis on *transparency*. Certainly, this helped investors, but it also benefited all employees, the collective *We*. Senior leaders communicated detailed findings of all wrongdoing, including Kozlowski's two million dollar Roman toga birthday party for his wife. Every time a new wrongdoing surfaced, company leaders made sure to inform those most affected.

Pillmore knew that the company needed to demonstrate its change of direction in ethical standards, but he also knew this effort required a culture change involving all stakeholders—the collective *We*. As the town halls continued over several years, Pillmore shifted from addressing the concerns of the *I*s to the collective concerns of the *We*. In December 2002, Governance Metrics, Inc., a corporate accountability ratings firm, rated Tyco a 1.5 on a scale of 1–10 and concluded it was one of the five worst companies globally. Pillmore made it clear that the members of the company must work together to raise awareness and accountability across the whole organization to address Tyco's ethical challenges.

Pillmore said the more he brought the need to the attention of the people of Tyco, the scores kept going up. Employees joined together to make the needed changes. By 2007, Tyco became one of 38 companies out of 3,800 to score a perfect 10. The problem could not be addressed only in the corporate office but in the daily transactions of the people of Tyco (the *We*) conducting its business, as well.

Healing the *It*

When an organization or team experiences trauma, survival becomes the short-term mission, but leaders must also set a new direction. The most urgent aspect of directional change for a company or team with misconduct, is culture. This powerful direction-setting tool guides the company in *how we will operate going forward to prevent a repeat of past mistakes*. In the opening months, senior leaders agreed that everything in the company would now operate within four values: *Integrity, Excellence, Accountability,* and *Teamwork*. The leadership team insisted that all employees hold all their leaders accountable to work within these values.

A major test occurred when compliance officers discovered new areas of ethical compromise. One manager embezzled seven million dollars over a five-year period and was arrested trying to flee the country. With prosecutorial help from the company, the manager went to jail. Another manager complained that he was being held accountable for sales targets that could only be reached by trading in the black market. This manager's disclosure precipitated a major review of how sales goals were set and how the company could operate successfully within white markets.

As the company rediscovered its bearings, Pillmore said, "We empowered leaders to recognize people. We gave awards to folks for a variety of things when they demonstrated the values in their work." This and other affirmations breathed Words of Life into the soul of the corporation. Of all the major companies that experienced major ethical and criminal compromises during that era, Tyco was the only company to survive.

Pillmore pointed out that Tyco's revenues never declined from the day of the crisis forward. They continued to rise, and, "We generated close to five billion in cash three years into the turnaround. We generated only five hundred million the year of the crisis." Pillmore and his colleagues in senior leadership roles at Tyco clearly brought out the best in their organization.

Conclusion

Whether steady state or responding to a disabling crisis, great team leaders must respond to and balance the needs of the *I*, the *We*, and the *It*. Transformational leaders breathe Words of Life into the core of the team and even the whole organization, as in the case of Tyco. Legendary organizations get this right.

Notes

1. My first exposure to this model occurred when I read Ruth Cohen's unpublished paper in graduate school. Professor Pauline Rose Clance distributed the paper to our class in the Department of Psychology at Georgia State University.

2. https://twitter.com/biiimurray/status/616298474812911616?lang=en.

9 Motivating High Potentials

The Four Transformations to Extraordinarily Influence the Best

My wife, Anne, and I call him Saint Ted. We are incredibly grateful that he stepped into our older son's life during a crucial developmental period. We believed Jim had tremendous potential to achieve a very high orbit in his life, and we did all that we could to help him fulfill that potential. However, there are some things that even the most well-intentioned parents cannot do for their children, and at those times, every parent prays that some important role model will step into the gap and help their child through a vital life transition. Saint Ted was the answer to our prayers.

Every year, Mr. Benning chose a couple of young guys to work for his highly regarded construction company. One night during Christmas break of Jim's first year of college, Mr. Benning called Jim and gave him the coveted invitation to work for him during the next summer after he completed his freshman year. Jim jumped at the chance and looked forward to the summer when he could don a hard hat and boots and work with the cool, big guys as they build impressive commercial structures.

Some vitally important life traits are better caught than taught. Emotional resilience is one of those. Understanding the dictionary definition does nothing to build those fibers of strength so vitally needed for a successful life. Anne and I were proud of all that Jim had accomplished to date and believed his trajectory was sound, but we also knew that new and more complex life challenges awaited him around the corner. There was no way Jim could anticipate the depth of resilience he would eventually need to be effective in the demanding world of business, and as a husband and father. Our only hope was that meaningful adversity would be served up in small enough courses that he would learn to bounce back and not become discouraged or disenfranchised as many young men do in our society. Mr. Benning believed part of his life mission was to use his company to build resilience in young men who sometimes missed the opportunity because of the ease with which many young people grow up today.

Jim showed up for work at the home office with his new work boots ready to go build a building. Mr. Benning wanted Jim to get some additional experience in the "working with his hands department" first. Next to the home office, a huge field reached toward the horizon. It was so overgrown with tall weeds you couldn't see across it. Mr. Benning's first job for Jim was to clear the entire lot of weeds—with a sickle—an assignment that took nearly two weeks. The first day, Jim came home so dirty and mad, he was beside himself. He immediately laid plans to quit and get what he thought would be a better job. Fortunately, he went back the next day. After two weeks of weed clearing, Jim was ready to receive his hard hat with the company logo and get to the real job.

Mr. Benning had other skills he felt Jim needed to master before moving up the corporate ladder. Jim spent the next two weeks using a hand-held scraper to remove peeling paint from a galvanized storage building. Each day Jim seemed to come home dirtier and more tired than the day before. It reminded me of the first *Karate Kid* movie where Mr. Miyagi required Daniel to perform an endless series of mundane physical tasks before he would train him to fight.

Every Friday, Mr. Benning asked Jim to stop by his office on Friday afternoon to give him a report on his progress. During these chats, Mr. Benning also talked about life, work, faith, and other topics he felt to be important in building a meaningful and successful life. Jim would sometimes give us a glimpse of what Mr. Benning said, and later, Anne and I would privately celebrate what Jim was learning. A particularly profound question Mr. Benning posed to Jim each Friday about his work was, "Is this the best you can do?" Jim interpreted the question not as a criticism, as in the quality of his work was poor. Rather, it posed a challenge to Jim to always measure himself against high standards.

On the fourth Friday, after a month of grueling manual labor, Jim graduated, and Mr. Benning gave him an official company hard hat. Monday morning, he was to report to a local job site, and "Goat" would be his supervisor. Jim's smile said it all when he came home. I've now arrived and get to hang out with the cool guys on a real construction site. He also received a small raise in his hourly wages.

At that point, Jim didn't know that the new guy must do the stuff no one else wants to do like shovel the loose gravel from the curbing and scrape dried cement from the places it spilled. Jim also learned the significance of his supervisor's name—Goat was not a paragon of interpersonal sensitivity. Jim's skin became thicker by the day.

Over the summer break, we gradually saw a beautiful quality emerging in Jim's life—emotional resilience—the ability to spring back from disappointment or adversity. None of us knew at the time how much Jim would eventually need resilience and other essential attributes.

Another benefit of Jim's summer job included working with and learning to respect some guys who had not and never would go to college; they might not have understood the details of the laws of physics, but they used the principles every day to build a quality building. They also worked hard in less than ideal circumstances—heat, humidity, dust, and danger. The great irony is that Jim now works as a real estate developer and builds commercial buildings. When he talks to guys on the construction crew, he understands their world. They respect the authenticity of his background.

The best part of the summer continued—the Friday afternoon chats with Mr. Benning. As he prepared to return to college, Jim was different. He had grown and the new school year showed it. He earned a starting position on the football team. His grades went up, and there was a new maturity and depth to him. The distractions he pursued during his freshman year no longer held such sway in his life. The unique difference Mr. Benning made in helping Jim to develop is why we call him Saint Ted.

A Great Test for Leaders

One of the great tests of leadership is the development of other leaders. The senior leaders of most organizations that I've served over the years know that some subset of their workers is more talented, smart, clever, hard-working, and has better people skills than others. It's not that other members don't make a significant contribution to the organization's mission, but some simply stand out. The strongly held belief is that senior leaders should expend extra time, energy, and money to make a difference in the lives of these gifted members. The conundrum for senior leaders is what to do differently with them and for them.

Many organizations refer to these individuals as *high-potential employees/leaders* or *HiPos*. As a rule of thumb, they are typically thought to be promotable at least two levels above their present position in a shorter period than normal. The general view is that HiPos should be given an enriched or higher octane set of job experiences and development or training resources to prepare them for bigger jobs in the future. While there are no guarantees that the investment will earn a dividend, paying special attention to these gifted members of the organization builds a pipeline of leadership talent vital to survival. Keeping and growing leadership talent constitutes a compelling need most organizations view as an indisputable need. The other convincing argument for developing younger high potential leaders is that they are significant retention risks. Word gets out. HiPos receive more calls from recruiters, and when a young leader is supplied with a steady stream of developmental opportunities, this provides strong reasons to stay put.

The question this chapter poses is how to exert extraordinary influence on these innately gifted individuals to bring out the best in them. Years ago, I conducted a research study and asked CEOs of large companies, "What was the most significant developmental experience you had on the way to becoming CEO?" I theorized that CEOs would place tremendous stock in their MBA or their extensive training, but what they unanimously agreed upon was their experience in different jobs. The challenge of the job itself was important, but what really made the job experience meaningful was the boss he or she had in each job—the unique influence of a boss who cared about their development! This chapter posits what we must do to bring out the best in those especially gifted individuals over whom we have influence.

Four Transformational Actions to Bring Out the Best in HiPos

In addition to whatever technical skills might be important to acquire, there are four actions we must take to accelerate our HiPos' development.

1. Affirm HiPos Style and Competence but Especially Their Core

- The numerous benefits of affirmation, based on scientific research, are amazingly high-octane fuel for HiPos. The list of benefits detailed in "Amazing Reasons to Affirm Your HiPos" contains an extraordinary set of qualities for aspiring senior leaders.

- Give HiPos Words of Life, as described in Chapter 4.

- Provide frequent Alliance Feedback and be sure to connect the feedback to HiPos' personal aspirations—their hopes and dreams.

- Encourage self-affirmation. I am not suggesting we promote narcissism or conceit, but the benefits of positive self-affirmation are considerable (nearby list). We foster self-affirmation by asking questions like, "Tell me what you feel you did well in the meeting today."

Amazing Reasons to Affirm Your HiPos

Brain research suggests a number of unique benefits of affirmation for HiPos.[1] While these benefits can manifest for anyone, leaders should seek to ensure their HiPos receive an enriched diet of affirmation with the following benefits:

- Promotes psychological well-being and mental health and makes their present work more meaningful.[2]

- Evokes calmness and positive emotions.[3]

- In combination with increased parasympathetic nervous system activity, positive emotions (by inference) are associated with hormones that foster trust and attachment and improve well-being.[4]

- Fosters physical well-being, including immune health, cardiovascular health, and hormone balance.[5]

- Better interpersonal relationships.[6]

- Positive work outcomes, such as a more active participation in the work process, facilitation of positive communication, and increased career satisfaction.[7]

- Fosters openness to new ideas.[8,9,10]

- Promotes positive self-worth or self-confidence, a critical attribute in executive success.[11]

- Reduces stress and improves higher cognitive thinking and problem-solving.[12,13,14]

- Made participants more persistent and increased their self-control during a tedious task, thus making the self-affirmer more efficient.[15]

- Fosters greater open-mindedness to opposing sides of an argument, more objectiveness when it came to hearing arguments that went against their own core beliefs, and better ability to deal with challenging arguments.[16,17]

- Made individuals more likely to accept feedback about negative behaviors such as poor health choices.[18]

- Increases self-esteem and, by inference, self-confidence.[19]

- Reduced susceptibility to the deleterious effects of stress.[20,21,22]

2. Encourage HiPos to Actively Build and Guard Their Core

An ancient king said, "Guard your core, because it determines the course of your life."[23] While a leader possesses many attributes for success, I believe with every fiber of my being that a strong core comprises the most important element of great leadership. The condition of our core determines the course of our lives, in general, and our effectiveness as a leader, in particular.

Over the last 10 years, I studied the leaders we most admire and those who conversely went down a path of personal destruction. In most cases, a strong core is the differentiator between those who build a great legacy versus those who end up in cataclysmic failure such as those who were fired from their organization because of a breach of their core. For more detail on the topic of leader derailment, I documented six CEOs whose boards fired them for a compromised core in an earlier book.[24]

The risks of derailment are greater for the gifted.

In my observation, the stages of derailment are predictable. Knowing these five stages and how to protect ourselves from the forces that drive us toward derailment at each stage are especially critical for a high-potential leader to understand. *The risks of derailment are greater for the gifted.*

Stage 1: Lack of Self Awareness. Lack of self-awareness is a common denominator among derailed leaders. When we lack self-awareness, it reflects a failure to recognize, understand, and regulate the forces operating inside us. High-potential leaders must cultivate the skills to know themselves and self-govern wayward impulses.

Frequent and intentional introspection and honest self-examination are vital means to self-awareness. Most of the successful CEOs I know keep a journal. They take notes throughout the day and reflect later on their handling of the events of the day. These reflections peel back the covers of blind spots and sometimes even go down the stairs to the basement of our darker motives.

HiPos should relish feedback from important others. They must seek it out and ask for candid observations from others to get better. They use feedback to calibrate how they are performing vis-a-vis expectations.

Stage 2: Arrogance. By definition, HiPos ride on the fast track. Power, position, status, fame, influence, money, and success often arrive sooner and in larger quantities for these individuals. Individually and especially collectively, these elements potentially create arrogance. *Arrogance is the mother of all derailers.* After great victories on the battlefield, Roman generals rode triumphantly into Rome amidst throngs of celebrants. A slave accompanied each general on his chariot and whispered over and over to the victorious general, "Fame is fleeting."

HiPos must stay grounded about any success. They need to be reminded over and over that *humility is the mother of all safeguards.* One CEO told me that in his organization, anyone who took too much credit for an outcome and didn't acknowledge the contributions of the team, "Got cut from the herd pretty quickly by other members of the organization."

> *Arrogance is the mother of all derailers. Humility is the mother of all safeguards.*

Stage 3: Missed Warning Signals. One senior executive I interviewed at a major U.S. company said, "I worry about getting caught up in my own importance and missing what I should be doing in leading my company and serving its members. I could easily wake up one morning blind to the path I followed to my own personal destruction." This statement reflects a profoundly admirable acknowledgement of the vulnerabilities any successful person faces.

Most executives who derail had plenty of warning signs that they ignored along the way. Derailment rarely occurs because of a single cataclysmic event, but rather as the consequence of a succession of small compromises over time. A calamitous event may trigger a derailment, but usually much was going on before its occurrence. If we groom high-potential leaders, we need to keep very short feedback loops. We may need to interpret subtle cues in the organization that otherwise would be missed.

The executive level frequently operates via a set of unwritten rules. A mentor guides HiPos to pay attention to cues and not run afoul of the opaque rules that exist in many organizations.

Derailment rarely occurs because of a single cataclysmic event, but rather as the consequence of a succession of small compromises over time.

Stage 4: Rationalization.   I like to think of *rationalize* as *rational lies*. Occasionally, we tell ourselves untruths, and these rational sounding *lies* lodge in our core as beliefs. As we said in Chapter 4, these beliefs guide our actions.

There are some lies to which HiPos are especially susceptible—lies that leaders love. Here are a few examples:

1. I am the smartest person in the room.

2. I am not subject to the normal rules that govern most people.

3. I am irreplaceable.

4. I add the greatest value to the endeavor.

If these four and a host of others take root in our core, it's just a matter of time before we head down that terrible path. Take number one, for example. This belief drips with arrogance. It causes overconfidence. It makes the holder of this belief contemptuous or disrespectful of those he or she views as inferior intellectually or of lesser value to the organization. The second rationalization led Tyco's Dennis Kozlowski to his catastrophic downfall.

Stage 5: Derailment.   Stage 5 arguably constitutes the point of no return. Once a leader becomes heavily invested in rationalization, an impenetrable wall seems to go up. Logic and moral clarity become irrelevant. Recently, I watched a several-year-old *60 Minutes* interview, during which Mike Wallace talked with Dennis Kozlowski at his prison. All Kozlowski discussed was his belief that the reasons the jury convicted him were simply wrong. He attempted to explain why taking hundreds of millions of dollars in "compensation" that the board of directors had not approved was justified—a truly dazzling display of rationalization on his slide to derailment.

***HiPos Have the Same Backgrounds and Credentials as Those who
Derail.*** As we mentor HiPos, it seems especially important to point
out that the leaders who derail are not fundamentally different from
us. For the most part, they grew up in reasonably normal families. They
went to college, then later to business school for an MBA and worked
their way up the corporate ladder. Then, wealth, fame, or power, or any
combination of the three, eroded his or her core. The protective walls
no longer protected them from arrogance and rationalization. A perfectly good person begins to act on those errant beliefs and starts moving through the stages of derailment.

The stories of most leaders who derail do not get splashed across
the front page of the *Wall Street Journal.* Rather, the leader derailment
occurs more quietly and without fanfare. None the less, a person with
extraordinary promise slips into the shadows of disgrace.

The most important role a leader plays in bringing along promis-
ing, talented leaders is to help them place a priority on guarding their
core. To accomplish this, the leader must also possess a strong core.
Speaking truth to another, just as with Words of Life, requires we lead
from a strong core. Otherwise, the mentor's hypocrisy and lack of
authenticity torpedo any opportunity for extraordinary influence in
another person's life.

3. Urge HiPos to Lead from Influence and Not from Position Power

When I meet with CEOs, I often tell them position power is overrated!
After publishing one of my earlier books, I called a friend who was
CEO of a huge consumer products company and asked him to
help me get my new book into his stores. I considered him to be an
outstanding role model for great leadership and thought, for sure, he
would be able to make this happen with a phone call.

His answer surprised me. He first said, "I honestly don't know
how that process works, whereby a book is approved for sales in our

stores." Second, "If I called the head of that department, she would be very respectful to me, but say something like, 'We really appreciate so much your interest in getting great books into our stores, and it sounds like you have a good candidate for us to consider. Our books do well because we have a process that gets on our shelves the exact books our customers want.'" My friend explained that this was a very polite way of saying, "You do your job, and we'll do ours." We both laughed, and he added, "By the way, if I tell her I want your book in the stores no matter what, she will do it, but your book will be doomed from the start. They will resent my exercise of power and will ensure it does not get the placement it needs to be successful."

Leaders must thoughtfully place HiPos in positions that require they learn to lead by influence and not by position power. When my younger son finished business school and took his first civilian job after leaving the U.S. Navy, his company placed him in a role that I thought was brilliant. While in the Navy, he commanded a unit with 40 sailors. The military, of course, stresses position power for understandable reasons, although I hear from experts that even the military feels many units, such as special operators, deemphasize hierarchical forms of leadership.

When he accepted his first position in a large corporation, management assigned profit and loss responsibility to him for a large business unit spanning North America. They tasked him with the coordination of five different functions in the business unit; however, no one reported directly to him. He needed the cooperation of a variety of people in various functions but with no formal authority to lead them. The structure forced him to lead through influence, collaboration, and alignment with the mission, values, goals, and culture of the organization.

After four years in this position, he was promoted to a management role, which included direct reports, but he had learned a vital lesson. It's far better to lead through influence than position power.

He learned how to lead with influence because he had no other form of power to use. Even though technically he now has position power, he elects to use it sparingly, because some very wise leaders in his company ingrained in him the importance of leading through influence.

We want to mentor our HiPos to lead with influence for one main reason. It engages those workers we lead to adopt higher levels of commitment to the mission, strategies, and goals. It creates ownership, whereby followers take ownership of the outcomes.

4. Help HiPos Develop Courage

Our affirmation of someone we mentor is highly effective in transforming that person, especially when we speak Words of Life into their core. In particular, we want to foster the development of courage, a vital attribute for senior management roles.

An influential leader called me recently and confided that, to this day, he regrets his failure to act while serving on a board of a highly visible and powerful U.S. company. The CEO of the company, by all accounts, was having an affair with his executive assistant. He was married, had two children in college, with one child still at home. The CEO was quite well regarded in his industry. Company earnings were consistently good, and the company was a darling of Wall Street.

Several board members talked privately with the CEO. His assistant traveled with him frequently on the company plane for no obvious business reason, but he assured them nothing was going on, despite the rumors and constant innuendos.

The subject was finally broached at a tension-filled board meeting, and the CEO said, "Fine, I resign," and stormed out of the board room. Board members sat quietly, until one said, "We have to get him back in the room and calm him down. He may be a flawed human being, but we need his leadership."

Two years later, company earnings tanked and company morale sunk to an all-time low. The CEO resigned after a prominent media outlet broke the story of his affair and the associated turmoil.

The man with whom I spoke said, "I didn't have the courage in that earlier board meeting to say what many of us felt. I should have said, 'I move we accept his resignation.'"

When I asked him why he didn't speak up, he said, "I was afraid."

"Of what?" I asked.

"Of being ostracized or removed from the board. I knew he might ask for my resignation if I went up against him, and no one would come to my rescue. I valued the prestige of being on a board of this well-known company … and the board member fees were significant."

We do not want to get cut from the herd, and our need for acceptance is one of the most powerful forces on the planet. We struggle and toss and turn worrying about what to do, even though in our gut, we know what we should do.

By the very nature of the job, leaders must take risks, yet as in this story, many factors discourage risk-taking. G. K. Chesterton said, "The paradox of courage is that a man must be a little careless of his life even in order to keep it."[25] We discussed earlier in the book how certain parts of our brains prefer safety and work to avoid risks. The word *encouragement* is derived from the French word *encoragier,* which means to put courage and heart into another.[26] Our HiPos will not achieve their potential without developing courage. To develop great leaders, we must encourage them. Words of Life result in the *encouragement* of the recipient.

Whether an executive who we believe can rise to a position of great influence, a gifted student, or an athlete with that rare potential for greatness, it is our privilege to help that person reach their potential. We must exert extraordinary influence to bring out the best in them!

We now turn our attention to a huge problem in the corporate world and in other endeavors, as well. Chapter 10 examines how we can bring out the best through more formal means of feedback, such as the dreaded annual performance review. There must be a better way!

Notes

1. Note to reader: Much of the scientific literature addresses the topic of self-affirmation. By inference, these benefits are thought to be derived from others' affirmation, as well.

2. K. A. Arnold et al., "Transformational Leadership and Psychological Well-Being: The Mediating Role of Meaningful Work," *Journal of Occupational Health Psychology* 12 (2007): 193–203.

3. A. I. Jack et al., "Visioning in the Brain: An fMRI Study of Inspirational Coaching and Mentoring," *Social Neuroscience* 8, no. 4 (2013): 369–384.

4. R. E. Boyatzis, K. Rochford, and S. N. Taylor, "The Role of the Positive Emotional Attractor in Vision and Shared Vision: Toward Effective Leadership, Relationships, and Engagement," *Frontiers in Psychology* 6 (2015), doi:10.3389/fpsyg.2015.00670.

5. Ibid.

6. A. Passarelli, "Vision-Based Coaching: Optimizing Resources for Leader Development," *Frontiers in Psychology* 6 (2015): 412.

7. Ibid.

8. G. L. Cohen, J. Aronson, and C. M. Steele, "When Beliefs Yield to Evidence: Reducing Biased Evaluation by Affirming the Self," *Personality and Social Psychology Bulletin* 26, no. 9 (2000): 1151–1164, doi:10.1177/01461672002611011.

9. G. L. Cohen and D. K. Sherman, "The Psychology of Change: Self-Affirmation and Social Psychological Intervention," *Annual Review of Psychology* 65 (2014): 333–371, doi:10.1146/annurev-psych-010213-115137.

10. D. B. Sherman, J. D. Creswell, and L. Jaremka, "Psychological Vulnerability and Stress: The Effects of Self-Affirmation on Sympathetic Nervous System

Responses to Naturalistic Stressors," *Health Psychology* 28, no. 5 (2009): 554–562.

11. G. L. Cohen, J. Garcia, N. Apfel, and A. Master, "Reducing the Racial Achievement Gap: A Social-Psychological Intervention," *Science* 313, no. 5791 (2006): 1307–1310, doi:10.1126/science.1128317.

12. J. D. Creswell, J. M. Dutcher et al., "Self-Affirmation Improves Problem-Solving Under Stress," *PLOS One* 8, no. 5 (2013).

13. J. D. Creswell, W. T. Welch et al., "Affirmation of Personal Values Buffers Neuroendocrine and Psychological Stress Responses," *Psychological Science* 16, no. 11 (2005): 846–851.

14. D. B. Sherman et al., "Psychological Vulnerability and Stress."

15. B. J. Schmeichel and K. Vohs, "Self-Affirmation and Self-Control: Affirm-ing Core Values Counteracts Ego Depletion," *Journal of Personality and Social Psychology* 96, no. 4 (2009): 770–782, doi:10.1037/a0014635.

16. G. L. Cohen, J. Aronson et al., "When Beliefs Yield to Evidence."

17. G. L. Cohen and D. K. Sherman, "The Psychology of Change."

18. E. B. Falk, M. B. O'Donnell et al., "Self-Affirmation Alters the Brain's Response to Health Messages and Subsequent Behavior Change," *Proceedings of the National Academy of Sciences USA* 112 (2015): 1977–1982.

19. G. L. Cohen, J. Garcia et al., "Reducing the Racial Achievement Gap."

20. J. D. Creswell, J. M. Dutcher et al., "Self-Affirmation Improves Problem-Solving."

21. J. D. Creswell, W. T. Welch et al., "Affirmation of Personal Values."

22. D. B. Sherman et al., "Psychological Vulnerability and Stress."

23. King Solomon, Proverbs 4:23, *New Living Translation* (author's paraphrase).

24. Tim Irwin, *DeRailed: Five Lessons Learned from Catastrophic Failures of Lead-ership* (Nashville, TN: Thomas Nelson, 2014).

25. G. K. Chesterton, from the essay "The Methuselahites," in *All Things Con-sidered: A Collection of Essays*, first published by Methuen & Co., London, 1908.

26. The Online Etymology Dictionary, http://www.etymonline.com/index.php?term=encourage.

10 Performance Appraisals that Lead to Extraordinary Influence

How One Famous Company Threw Out Its Traditional Performance Appraisal System and the New Process That's Reaping Big Gains

A client asked a colleague to meet with a senior executive who had been the object of numerous complaints over the years. His value to the company was quite significant due to his industry knowledge and extensive technical skills. The loss of his contributions to the business threatened a huge setback in competitive advantage. The CEO asked my colleague to conduct a 360 exercise or what's also called multi-rater feedback. Despite many earlier failures to help this talented executive change his behavior, the deep hope of management was that holding up the mirror based on the anonymous feedback from his peers and direct reports would break through his hardened shell and motivate him to make needed changes in how he related to others. Although everyone agreed he would never be a bastion of interpersonal warmth in his business relationships, they hoped that his denigration of others who did not possess his technical prowess and industry expertise could be better controlled.

The feedback session did not go well. My colleague, a leading expert in this field, carefully navigated the landmines she knew covered the landscape of his psyche. Despite her focus on his remarkable strengths, he became increasingly agitated as the critical feedback surfaced on the report. It drew stark attention to his considerable maladies.

Beads of sweat appeared on her client's forehead. She politely asked if it was time for a break. Without warning, the man stood up abruptly. He grabbed the edges of the table and violently threw the table over with a huge crash. He then stormed out of the room. Fortunately, my colleague was sitting on the client's side of the table so that they could view the same copy of the report. After quickly contacting the CEO's office and HR, a hastily called meeting ensued, during which an early retirement package was assembled for a manager the company hated to lose.

While most performance feedback meetings don't go this badly, they are probably the most universally hated experiences in many organizations, both from the giver's and the receiver's perspective. I believe that in most cases, managers intend their feedback to improve employees' performance and increase their value to the organization. The reality is that most performance appraisals accomplish the exact opposite of what's intended. They close off communication and create stress and resentment on the receiver's part.

Romantic poet Elizabeth Barret Browning wrote a famous sonnet, "How Do I Love Thee? Let Me Count the Ways (Sonnet 43)," expressing her great affection for her husband, Robert Browning. Most members of the organizational community would like to write a reverse sonnet directed at their boss during performance appraisal season, "How Do I Hate Thee; Let Us All Count the Ways." A very long list ensues.

Here are opinions and comments I hear routinely from givers and receivers of performance evaluation:

- "My annual performance appraisal meetings with my boss are incredibly awkward and stressful."

- "My anxiety is off the charts. I feel so defensive, I don't hear a word."

- "How can you fairly capture a year's work into one rating—it is not a true picture of my performance."

- "I receive very little truly helpful and actionable information."

- "The whole process feels demeaning."

- "As a manager, it's the most cumbersome, time-consuming thing I do. It takes months to prepare them for all my direct reports and then prove to my boss that my ratings are fair. Candidly, it's a huge waste of time. I'd rather just talk with my direct reports every day or so."

- "While the recipient is supposed to hear a balanced view of their performance, he or she focuses only on the negative feedback."

- "A bad rating creates a lingering effect of decreased motivation. One survey said engagement drops 23% when an employee receives a lower rating than they feel they deserve."[1]

- "I could have solved world hunger in January, but my manager remembers only the minor dropped ball in December when he rates me."

  Author comment: Most feel performance ratings suffer from the "recency effect," "The tendency for individuals to be most influenced by what they have last seen or heard."[2]

- "I have a boss who's never given an Exceeds Expectations rating for the past 30 years. She maintains, 'I set my expectations correctly, so how is it possible to exceed them?' My friend's boss gives her Exceeds Expectations for the most average accomplishments."

  Author comment: Reliability across raters is notoriously poor.

- "I just play it safe to ensure I get a good rating and a raise."

  Author comment: How performance appraisal is frequently used discourages innovation.

Scott Adams had a field day with Dilbert around the comedy so inherent in performance reviews, as depicted in Figure 10.1.

How do we fix such a broken model? What must be re-engineered to make performance feedback meaningful? Based on what we learned about the brain in Chapter 4, it seems obvious that the basic premise of most performance appraisal systems throws the hyper defensive part of the brain (the amygdala) into overdrive.

Some large companies are addressing common problems with the traditional systems. For example, Microsoft, Lilly, GE, Dell, The Gap, Accenture, Adobe, New York Life, and other well-known companies are getting rid of rating categories.[3] Goldman Sachs, known for their

Figure 10.1 Dilbert Cartoon

Source: DILBERT © 1997 Scott Adams. Used by permission of Andrews McMeel Syndication. All rights reserved.

highly mathematical 1-to-9 scales, recently stopped rating employees with numbers.[4]

To make this topic much more accessible, I talked with a practitioner who led his company to radically rethink how performance appraisal works in his organization. It was my privilege to talk with the CEO of a highly admired company that has dramatically changed its process for employee performance appraisal. Michael (Mike) L. Ducker is chief executive officer and president of FedEx Freight Corporation. Mike served in a variety of other roles at FedEx, including the chief operating officer and president of international express freight services at Federal Express Corporation. Mike previously served as an executive vice president of international express freight services for FedEx Express.

I asked Mike why he wanted to change the traditional system of performance appraisal at FedEx Freight. He minced no words in saying, "People just hated it!" He added that the officer and director levels particularly hated it and found it very labor intensive and exhausting. Managers dreaded the end of the year when the forms had to be completed, and described it as "fruitless activity." According to them, it took a week of just "filling out squares."

Mike pointed out that another compelling reason the company "ditched the old system" was the negative cloud that hung over the experience for everyone involved. "We wanted to celebrate employees' success. We wanted to make it a much more positive and uplifting experience."

"We are in the service business, and we thrive depending upon the *discretionary effort* of every employee. It's just a different feeling when discretionary effort is present. This is crucial for us. You cannot recognize this vital competitive differentiator just filling in the boxes."

Mike strongly believes that, "Employees want to do a great job. Nobody puts on their uniform, walks out the door, drives to work

and says, 'I'm going to screw something up today.' Most people go
to work and think about how they can do a better job than they did
yesterday—they feel responsible and accountable for their actions. The
manager's job is to create an environment where people can succeed
and excel." According to Mike, the old performance appraisal form,
and more importantly the philosophy behind it, neither fostered nor
recognized these inherently positive inclinations of FedEx Freight's
employees.

Mike further espoused his philosophy of employees in saying,
"We hire the best and the brightest people. We give them a just
and fair place to work. We pay them commensurate wages with the
marketplace. We give them promotional opportunities, and as such,
we have always run some of the lowest turnover rates in the transportation industry. We believe that if we do those things well with our
employees, then our employees will make every customer experience
outstanding." The problem remained that the legacy performance
appraisal system was out of step with the company's philosophy of
people.

After Mike became CEO of FedEx Freight, he hired a new senior
officer of human resources, Jeff Greer. "One of the first assignments
I gave him was to ditch the performance system and develop a new one
that served the mission in a much more constructive manner." Jeff,
an attorney by background, began a total performance management
redesign project, involving his peers from the start.

A critical goal was to " … make it less formal and a lot less intimidating. We called it a 'performance chat' and significantly increased the
frequency from once a year to three times a year. We also stressed the
need for managers to have much more frequent conversations about
how employees were doing.

"We tied our new system to the foundational principles that have
made our company successful—people, service, profit. We review
these principles with our employees all the time. These three form a

'virtuous circle' that starts with people. If our employees are treated well, they give our customers an excellent experience, and then the customers reward us with more business and we make a profit—the virtuous circle. We reinvest that profit back in our people, back in our service, back in our company. The performance chat then revolves around the three elements of the virtuous circle. Additionally, we added two other categories: Development of Self and Development of Others to make a total of five categories, which form the 'platform' for discussion during our performance chat.

"Each of the five categories has specific subelements we discuss with our employees. For example, the people category includes interpersonal skills, collaboration, professionalism, hiring, and other facets. Conversation about profits would include budgets, efficiencies, costs, management of capital, etc. Managers guide the conversation through the topics but are expected to focus first on how the individual feels about his or her performance in various categories. The other point to emphasize again is that we want the frequency of the performance chat to increase dramatically. This includes the planned three times a year, but even more often on an informal basis."

One of my curiosities—is there a form? "Yes, but a very simple one and only one page that covers the five categories."

I also asked Mike how the performance chat stays connected to strategic priorities and other key expectations for a given job. Mike emphasized the company's fiduciary responsibility to FedEx shareholders. "The company determines a management by objectives program born out of the work of the strategic management committee at the holding company level. This committee reviews markets, competition, and company performance. The conclusions of this very detailed process are distilled into major corporate objectives. Some subset of these overarching corporate objectives is deemed relevant to each manager's functional responsibilities. The manager level and above have two 'platforms' reviewed in what are usually two different conversations. The first platform includes the five categories described earlier. The second platform for managers and above includes their subset of corporate objectives, which are tied directly to their bonus compensation."

It's quite normal to encounter resistance when changing a legacy process. For example, certain stakeholders mastered the existing approach or maybe embraced the philosophy of the way performance appraisal worked historically. Those stakeholders may view the old approach as the best means to hold members of the organization accountable or believe the new slant as too soft.

Some human resource organizations prefer a more compliance-oriented approach and want the system to provide accountability as well as careful documentation of employee performance. It would be quite normal for HR professionals with this orientation to resist an approach with less structure. They also might feel that the average manager may not possess the interpersonal savvy to effectively use an approach that does not have the configuration of a check-the-box form.

Mike reported that there was a celebration when they jettisoned the old system and introduced the new one. They experienced minimal pushback, and he attributes the positive reception to several factors. First, FedEx Corporation chairman Fred Smith was " … incredibly supportive. He is an innovator and welcomed the simplification." Second was Jeff Greer's leadership of the effort. Third was the inclusion of a variety of stakeholders, including those who may have been invested in a more compliance-oriented approach. When I asked Mike about any changes he would make in the process used to develop the new system, he said the involvement of key stakeholders was so valuable, he wished that he had included even more people.

Mike insisted that the legal team be involved. "It helped that Jeff Greer is an attorney himself, but the company's legal team participated from the outset." He also wanted assurance that any new system would include appropriate documentation, "should controversy occur." The system provides for a formal "performance improvement" process, as needed.

When I asked Mike how managers who prefer a more structured approach were adapting to the new system, he pointed out that built-in flexibility guides how it's used. Also, managers are required to provide one overall rating of each employee on a four-level scale:

1. Above Acceptable

2. Acceptable

3. Needs Improvement

4. Too New to Rate

Raters do not use numbers—only one of these four verbal categories listed. There is no forced distribution, in which a manager must divide the employees he or she rates in set percentages within each category. Mike added that if a manager rated 90% of his or her employees *Above Acceptable* and the unit was not reaching its strategic goals, then a conversation with the rating manager would ensue.

I asked Mike about training for managers in the use of the new system. For the initial launch, there were limited support materials. The company employs a highly talented learning and development group, which will soon implement a cutting-edge learning system with video and interactive modules.

FedEx Freight and other companies mentioned previously have clearly led the corporate world in innovation of new approaches to performance management. Legacy elements like check-the-box and elaborate numerical rating systems seem headed for the scrapyard of performance appraisal. The virtually universal hatred of most legacy systems forecasts a revolution over the next few years.

What Must Any Reinvention of Performance Feedback Include?

Because *Extraordinary Influence* speaks to how leaders transform members of their organizations, we should consider what principles and practices from this book might be incorporated in any rethinking of performance management.

Some elements of what I propose could be facilitated in a process or even a form. More important are the *perspectives* that leaders must adopt to truly transform the people they lead. *A check-the-box system may inform, but it will not transform.* Ultimately, a leader's transformational influence depends upon the *person of the leader*.

A check-the-box system may inform, but it will not transform.

I am a strong believer in the value of training; however, training alone will not make this approach work. Rather, it's the personal deepening of the leader who must learn to connect with his or her followers in a more substantive way. A leader's solid core makes transformation of others possible.

What are the perspectives and practices that I particularly value when an organization wants to reinvent its performance review system?

Timeliness

There are a few irrefutable laws of human behavior. One law maintains that the closer to the occurrence of a certain behavior feedback ensues, the more effective the feedback. There are many aspects of performance management that Mike Ducker and his team devised that contribute to a more effective system, but without doubt, one of the most profound changes is frequency. Why anyone thinks that a once a year meeting has any great value denies the inarguable principle that proximity of feedback to the behavior matters tremendously. I worked closely with the executive vice president of a highly regarded Fortune 500 company and asked her how often performance feedback should be given. She said, "Daily."

Affirmation of the Core

What is the primary door to the higher order brain functions that lead to innovation, creativity, and resilience? Affirmation. If we want to foster high performance, then affirm on the three levels described in detail in Chapter 4—customary style, competence, and core.

Brain science makes it certain that affirmation is the key to accessing the higher order centers of our brains. If we want to transform those we lead, our system must promote the use of affirmation. Regardless of how a form or a process is designed, affirming feedback must be central. Feedback needs to include *what* was done and *how* it was done. The *what* considers the leader's competence. The *how* considers the impact of a person's style as he or she accomplished the tasks and goals, worked with team members, or represented the organization in some fashion. The *who* we are reflects our core.

The most important opportunities for transformation occur in our core. Affirmation of someone's core is likely less frequent but highly impactful when given. Affirmation of style and conduct lend themselves to frequent feedback. Affirmation of a person's core is likely more opportunistic. To use FedEx Freight's term, a *performance chat* could be an opportune time to go deeper with someone and affirm his or her core.

To reach a person's core, we must speak *Words of Life*, the language of the core introduced in Chapter 4. What language does the core hear? Below are the 10 major examples of *Words of Life* that "light up our core!" A performance chat is an ideal time to mention one or several of these dimensions:

1. *Integrity*—"You handled that ethically challenging problem with great character. This was a great expression of our corporate values."

2. *Courage*—"You demonstrated tremendous courage in walking away from that legacy account. After you explained to our CEO, he understood the reasons and supported your decision."

3. *Humility*—"Although everyone knows you did the work, you publically attributed the success of the project to your team. It was a very selfless gesture on your part."

4. *Judgment*—"The way you navigated the decision to abandon the old IT platform was superb. Even the supporters of the old system said the way you led us to the conclusion displayed skill in arguing for the transition to the new system."

5. *Authenticity*—"Your openness and honesty about how you really felt about the new project helped the team avoid a bad misadventure."

6. *Self-regulation*—"Although you would have been fully justified in setting off a neutron bomb in that meeting with the marketing department, you showed great restraint, which helped get our program back on track."

7. *Wisdom*—"You made a decision to spend time that you didn't have on the West Coast cleaning up the mess that the software implementation team made. You saved a huge client and quietly mitigated what we all knew was a major blunder. The IT guys know they royally screwed up, but the way you handled this made them a friend for life."

8. *Candor*—"You spoke truth to power when you told our CEO that his new pet project could not be profitable for at least three

years, if ever. That was a risky move, but everyone else in the C suite expressed relief." Although our CEO was disappointed, he commended you for your candor.

9. *Resilience*—"Your resolve and flexibility made this project successful."

10. *Influence*—"We had to have the marketing folks on our team. Despite their view that our project was a lower priority, you won them over. Our client can't believe we got this project launched so quickly. They are delighted."

The *What, How,* and *Who* Dimensions Must Be Included in Any Reengineered Performance Management System

Most legacy systems focus on *what* a person accomplished. The *how* may sometimes be included, but, in my experience, the *who*, or those core dimensions already discussed, rarely are reflected in manager/employee feedback. The *who* is where true transformation occurs, but many leaders either do not know how to speak Words of Life or do not know how to achieve that level of interpersonal exchange.

Training and development in any new system are essential, especially when the changes involve moving into deeper connectedness with the core of subordinates. Chapter 4 provides a list of leader practices needed to speak effectively into another's core.

In Chapter 5, I made the case that based upon the newest brain science, constructive criticism or negative feedback engages a part of the brain that shuts down receptivity and problem-solving capabilities. Yet, anyone in leadership legitimately asks, how do you correct someone who performed badly or who needs to improve in certain areas of their job?

In Chapter 6, I suggested several conditions, that when met, help a person hear a contrary perspective on their work performance. Some might argue that we cannot coddle an employee who needs to take corrective steps. I argue simply from pragmatism that our feedback to employees is more likely to bear fruit when delivered in a way that can be heard and considered. This, in no way, precludes what Mike Ducker referred to as a "performance improvement" process. It does argue that if we want to transform an employee's work, a different approach than traditional criticism will produce better results.

Alliance Feedback builds on the premise that employees usually accept if not actively buy in to the goals of the team or department. We are better off talking with employees about actions that will bring them into greater alignment with the team's goals versus telling them they are getting a 3 on a 1–10 scale of performance. I am not a form designer, but a performance review form that reminds people of the plumb line of goals and strategic direction of the team would be extremely helpful in this instance.

Brain research makes it clear that the most powerful Alliance Feedback ties performance comments to the standard of an employee's personal hopes, dreams, and aspirations. In my observation, most performance appraisal systems include some discussion of an employee's development, that is, how he or she can improve. Tying development to the achievement of personal career goals connects with the parts of our brain responsible for innovation and resourcefulness. For example, we might say to a subordinate,

"If you collaborate more with your colleague on the marketing team, you will build a much more positive personal brand with her and in her department. Informal feedback from significant stakeholders around you figures prominently into who gets promoted to management in our company. Being more intentional in relationship building with your peers in other departments will help you achieve that important goal of joining the leadership team."

Some might argue that this example is too indirect. One might say, "Look, you blew it. When you had an opportunity to get Cindy's help on the project, you never once called her. That's why I'm giving you a

2 on cross-functional collaboration." While admittedly, this approach is more direct, the problem is that we know from brain science that the recipient shuts down. Any hope of transforming the person is lost. A large body of research supports the efficacy of connecting Alliance Feedback to something of value to the recipient.

For example, tying Alliance Feedback to the hopes and dreams of the recipients produces many positive reactions in the brain, such as calmness and openness to new ideas, the releasing of important brain chemicals, and even positive cardiovascular health.

Build Trust

Additional keys to make performance feedback effective are to have a foundation of trust and to be sure that the recipient of your feedback knows that, down deep, you are really "for them." This is particularly important when giving Alliance Feedback. Irritation or impatience torpedoes any chance of transformation. The amygdala goes into overdrive, thereby shutting down the positive channels of access you might have to someone's core. Trust deposits at every turn make it much more likely that a person will know that our motivation derives from commitment to their success. Reminding recipients of your feedback that you are truly for them and for their advancement in the organization works wonderfully with the way our brains are wired.

The CEOs I interviewed for this book stressed that every recipient of performance feedback needs to hear a blend of encouragement and challenge. The approach I'm advocating is not coddling of employees, as some more task-oriented critics might suggest. Challenging people we lead to perform better fits with every recommendation I offer in this book. I'm acting out of a desire to see the people in our organizations flourish. I'm not suggesting that the principles and perspectives advocated here will work with everyone, because there are people who simply do not belong in our organizations. A job is not rehab.

From a practical standpoint, we must be selective in those with whom we invest this intensively.

What I advocate is that we create cultures in our organizations that are truly developmental. Many companies that adopt this perspective in earnest achieve amazing results. They become places where people love to work. By any metric, these organizations outperform their competitors.

Performance management in various forms will remain a part of our best organizations. My strong hope is that those who redesign their organization's performance management systems will take full advantage of new brain research and thoughtfully consider how to bring out the best in those we lead!

Notes

1. https://www.wsj.com/articles/how-performance-reviews-can-harm-mental-health-1445824925.

2. http://www.encyclopedia.com/social-sciences/dictionaries-thesauruses-pictures-and-press-releases/recency-effect.

3. https://www.wsj.com/articles/how-performance-reviews-can-harm-mental-health-1445824925.

4. https://www.wsj.com/articles/goldman-sachs-dumps-employee-ranking-system-1464272443.

11 Special Counsel to Parents, Teachers, and Coaches

Extraordinary Influence for Those Entrusted to Our Care

For many years in January, I taught a graduate course at a school in Orlando. One of my students proposed we take a break from class early one afternoon to watch the launch of the Space Shuttle some miles away at Cape Canaveral. Even from that distance we could see the huge plumes of fire and smoke from the solid fuel rocket boosters during the liftoff. The students spontaneously broke into cheers and applause seeing this amazing sight. Although we could not physically see this stage, as the Space Shuttle neared the edge of space and weightlessness, the two solid booster engines broke away from the shuttle body and parachuted into the ocean. At that point, the on-board engines took over and propelled the Space Shuttle to its mission.

When our sons were growing up, we talked about how the Space Shuttle was a metaphor for what Anne and I believed to be our primary mission in their lives. We wanted most of all to provide them with a loving and safe home, but then also to do everything within our power to get our sons into the highest orbit possible. We did everything we knew to do to help our sons develop and grow academically, socially, athletically, spiritually, and personally. We tried to set high expectations from their earliest years. Before they were even aware of what a space shuttle was, they knew intuitively we expected them to pursue a high calling. Anne and I laugh today about the unfurnished living room in our home. Almost no sacrifice was too great to ensure that the boys had every opportunity to grow into their potential.

What we also told them was just like the solid rocket boosters, we would someday soon drop away and parachute into the ocean, metaphorically speaking. At that point, the on-board engines would have to take over. They would become fully responsible for themselves. They would have to use their own resources to propel their lives forward, including the wisdom and judgment to make good decisions. We would be cheering for them and awed by their future accomplishments but they were not to expect that Anne and I would be the source of propulsion.

The space shuttle may be a good metaphor for anyone who seeks to help children reach their potential. Certainly, parents want this for their children, but there are also teachers, coaches, religious leaders, and others who work with children and want those under their care to reach high and to learn to thrive on their own.

Courage to Fight for Our Children's Well-Being

Are we willing to fight for our children and to even risk their embarrassment to protect them? I will never forget the mother of one of Jim's high school football teammates who learned that her son (a future Division I player) earned a C on a math test. She stormed down to the practice field in high heels and walked into the middle of a live scrimmage after the play had already started. With bodies flying everywhere, she grabbed her son by the face mask and dragged him to the sidelines. She told him that he could not return to football practice until he made a better grade on the test. Under protest he immediately left football practice for after-school help still wearing his pads. The most entertaining part of the story is that all the coaches stood silently huddled together on the sideline watching the spectacle unfold; they were not about to question this high-expectation mom.

As my wife, Anne, came to be friends with this particular mom over the years, she learned that this family had a very strong *We*. They were clear about their values and strong cohesion as a family. The parents maintained a steely conviction that they would do everything possible to help their two sons become successful adults. They placed their family and its cohesion above all else. Their strong spiritual faith eliminated certain friends if they felt their influence might compromise the safety and well-being of their sons in any way. The son who was dragged off the field now commands a huge warship in the U.S. Navy.

Parents regularly face tests of courage over a willingness to be rejected by those whose approval and esteem we think we need. It might be telling a 14-year-old daughter, "No, you're not wearing that dress to the Holiday Dance." It might be, "I'm sorry my 12-year-old son can't come to the sleepover in your home, because we don't allow him to watch R-rated movies." We are not lacking for examples of tests, but the question for all parents is whether we can make the hard decisions when the values we hold paramount are tested.

Words of Life—The Fuel to Reach a High Orbit

As we discussed throughout this book, the power of affirmation is extraordinary, but it is especially influential in the lives of children. To raise healthy, accomplished children, we *must* affirm them. We must affirm them for their growing competence and especially, we must regularly speak Words of Life into our children's core to affirm their character.

One practice that we started in our family when our children were quite young was that on the family member's birthday (including parents, grandparents, etc.), each family member would say something they liked and respected about the birthday celebrant. Our two sons continued this practice with their children. It is truly amazing to watch the recipient hear Words of Life being spoken into their core. As the kids get older the profundity of their affirmation grows!

Important authority figures, teachers, and coaches play a tremendously important role in affirming the competence of students. When the opportunity is there, speaking Words of Life into a student's core can make a profound difference in a child's life. When coaches and teachers do speak Words of Life to their students and players, they can truly bring out the best in them. Speaking Words of Life to a child requires a parent, teacher, or coach to have an intact core themselves. Unfortunately, this is not always the case.

The Tragedy of Words of Death

Also powerful are the withering effects of criticism and shame—Words of Death. Parents, teachers, and coaches have tremendous potential to deliver damaging words to children. Important figures in our lives who are wounded in their own core often use criticism and shame to motivate a child, not because it's ultimately effective, but because it reflects the words spoken to them by a parent or some other influential person.

One man I observed coach for several years was unbelievably toxic and shouldn't have been allowed to be around children. Shame was his primary method of motivation. Even to the untrained eye, most of the players' parents knew something was amiss with his core. Why school administrators are not more discerning in vetting their coaching talent always surprises me and makes me question the administrator's competence.

As in my story about Anne's first grade teacher, we know how impressionable young children are. I can still see some of my coaches' degrading looks firmly lodged in some neuron in my own brain.

College Football: An Amazing Laboratory Experiment

Abusive coaching is certainly not new to college sports. In fact, allegations of abuse are appearing with increasing frequency, even in the sports with fewer followers. For coaches, a transition from abuse to affirmation may be difficult when the stress is high, and many coaches know that too many losses may cost them their job. An important article in *Sports Illustrated* suggests that even college football coaches may now be seeing the world differently when it comes to harsh criticism.[1]

Dr. Barbara Fredrickson, the author of *Positivity* and a social psychologist who runs the Positive Emotions and Psychophysiology (PEP) Lab at the University of North Carolina, says, "Negative emotions grab people's attention more … there's a perception that the best way to get what you want out of employees or players is by negativity or threats, or being stressful or intense. But in terms of bonding, loyalty, commitment to a team or a group and personal development over time, negativity doesn't work as well as positivity."[2]

Dr. Ben Tepper of Ohio State's Fisher College of Business says, "The studies all say there's no incremental benefit to being hostile." Abusive coaching does not lead to increased strength and cohesion of the team. It's draining and divisive. Over time, research will discredit abusive coaching strategies. Tepper further notes, "Even when you control for a leader's experience and expertise, hostility always produces diminishing returns."[3]

I sometimes ask parents why we yell at our kids, and I usually get a blank stare. Why do managers, coaches, and parents still employ harsh criticism and yelling as a preferred way to motivate? The short answer—it works. As Fredrickson's words suggest, if nothing else, harsh words get our attention, but there is a big problem with using negativity as a motivational tactic.

Criticism fails the sustainability test, and it needs escalation to continue to be effective. I've always thought it strange that parents count to three to get young children into compliance. The parent's voice intensity and volume increases over the short cadence, and the kid learns quickly that you do nothing until his or her parent reaches *three*. The parent becomes the one whose behavior is controlled in this instance! More importantly, yelling does nothing to develop a self-reliant, self-regulated child.

Likewise, being critical of an employee gets short-term results but does little to develop a mature, self-directed worker. We get results from criticism, but it invariably fails to bring about lasting transformation and maturity in those who are the recipients of this approach. Criticism, even when the manager fully believes his or her motives for the feedback are fully positive, fails to produce the results he or she seeks over a long period of time.

By the way, I don't claim to be a paragon of virtue here. When my sons were younger, I gave my share of high intensity speeches in an attempt to get them in line. The only lasting value of my speeches is the boys' parody of what I said way back then. Of course, I'm always the goat in the embellished retelling of my most famous speeches. *Parent alert*—when we're under stress, what we say to our children may hurt them, but it may also become their best comedy material when they are older!

Parent alert—*when we're under stress, what we say to our children may hurt them, but it also may become their best comedy material when they are older!*

Alliance Feedback for Children

Because brain science has settled that criticism does not bring out the best in another person, especially a child, how do we correct errant behavior? The concept of Alliance Feedback, introduced in Chapter 6, provides a powerful way to redirect a child's behavior.

Alliance Feedback is the connecting of behaviors needing improvement to the hopes, dreams, and aspirations of the recipient.

In Chapter 2, I mentioned my outstanding math teacher in high school, Mrs. Chapman. I remember reviewing a math test with her on which I earned a terrible grade. I'll never forget when she looked up and said with the utmost respect and concern, "You are so much better than this." In that short, pithy phrase, I heard, "You have the potential to go somewhere with your life. With more focused effort on this subject, you can prepare yourself for a much bigger impact. Don't squander your talent through this kind of mediocrity." In the months that followed, I made the effort and went to before-school help sessions many days a week. Mrs. Chapman set in motion certain attitudes that guide me still, many decades later.

Parents, teachers, and coaches should be primary sources of Alliance Feedback versus criticism. If a child dreams of being an astronaut, doctor, engineer, teacher, minister, or entrepreneur, connect that aspiration with any errant behavior, such as not doing their homework. Connect anything a child does that needs to be corrected to a relevant hope or dream. This is a scientifically grounded phenomenon!

Alliance Feedback avoids criticism, and instead, points out the incongruity between something a child wants and the way they are acting. For a high school student, it may be as simple as saying, "You said you want to attend college at (name of school). We support you in that goal but question whether making a C in physics (your current grade) will hurt your chances for admission."

Anne and I were called into a parent conference with the principal one morning just before Christmas break during Jim's senior year in high school (fortunately, our first conference of this nature). Jim chose to apply early decision to his first choice for college and learned in early December he'd been accepted for admission, assuming he finished high school.

The principal didn't beat around the bush. He looked at Jim and said, "Congratulations on getting into college early decision. Unfortunately, your grades have fallen into precipitous decline since receiving that good news. Football seems to be the only thing that matters to you right now. I want you to know that if your grades do not return to the level that your college used to evaluate you for admission, I am obligated to inform the admissions officer that you no longer meet their academic standards. He has the right to rescind your acceptance." Jim's eyes were now big as saucers, and he was uncharacteristically speechless. The principal was not critical, but he used Alliance Feedback to profound effect. For the rest of the school year, he was a model student. Sometimes life lessons are *better caught that taught.*

Sometimes life lessons are better caught that taught.

The boys tease me often and have funny labels for some of my more memorable parenting speeches. Some of the ones I delivered under the duress of them acting badly cannot be mentioned in polite society! My *vacuum speech* stressed that they needed to learn to discipline themselves and be self-regulating. Otherwise, somebody else would fill the vacuum created by their lack of self-control. It might be a teacher, a coach, the principal, a boss, or even the police, but nature abhors a vacuum! Filling the control vacuum themselves would always be more pleasant than when some grumpy authority figure stepped into the vacuum to fill it for them. Jim's high school principal filled the vacuum when his senior year grades took a plunge, and it was not pleasant. It was effective, though, and it was applied without an ounce of criticism.

The *I*, *We*, and *It* for Families

In Chapter 8, we looked at the "I, We, It" model. In our family, we sought to maintain a balance among the *I*, the *We*, and the *It*. Because I believe this model has such broad applicability in life, it behooves parents, teachers, and coaches to be intentional about keeping these three aspects in balance in the home, at school, and on teams, clubs, and so on.

How does this model apply to a family? Parents first need to encourage the development of the *I* for each child. Find out something the child is good at doing and help him or her get better. I am a strong believer in lessons—piano, gymnastics, karate, chess, and even individual lessons for team sports like baseball. Finding someone in the community who teaches batting lessons or pitching lessons helps the child have a better chance of excelling.

Academic tutoring can also be helpful. The world is more competitive, and reality dictates that we seek to give our children every opportunity to excel. This includes counseling for a child who might be fearful or generally lacking in confidence. We recognized that our two sons were different and needed different developmental opportunities. We tried to encourage each child to use their strengths and to grow in areas that we believed would become important in the future.

The Family *We*

The family's sense of *We* is foundational. The family provides a natural training ground for the *We* to develop. Every family, regardless of the composition of two parents, one parent, one parent and a grandmother, and so on, has an opportunity to create a narrative for their unique family. The *We* provides a boundary within which a child is protected and distinctive.

There are also many opportunities for a child to experience a strong *We* outside of his or her family. For example, a sport's team is great preparation for a work team with all the interpersonal demands, conflict management, and social skills required to work and get along today.

Many diverse opportunities in a child's life require a *We*, which become a wonderful opportunity to develop the skills for working with others. It might be a baseball or soccer team, a cheerleading squad, a robotics club, scouts, a community service group, a church youth group, and any number of other areas of involvement. A child may be unusually talented at some individual activity, which should be encouraged, but I believe it vital that this child be involved in some activity with a sense of *We*.

Excellent coaches develop individual players, for example, a lineman in football must be taught the correct footwork to be in position for an effective block of a defensive player; however, many sports also reflect the necessity of playing as a team. A great coach works relentlessly to build a strong sense of *We*, which is so vital to winning in team sports.

In our family, Anne and I worked particularly hard to help our sons learn how to get along with others—how to be on a team, and how to help and encourage others. We knew that emotional intelligence was as important as, if not ultimately more important than their IQ. They needed to be self-aware, empathetic, self-governing, and able to influence others. Their style of relating to others would determine much of any future success.

Parents must balance the amount of attention to the *I*, *We*, and *It* in a family. Sometimes the needs of an individual family member outweigh every other concern in a family, such as a child with an injury or illness. Even when a family must focus disproportionately on the needs of a single family member, it's important to keep a sense of the *We*.

The *It* of a Family or Team

I believe that when references are made to "the breakdown of the family unit" and the catastrophic consequences of this in our society, the issue being referred to has resulted from deterioration of a clear *It* for the family. We've largely lost the sense of purpose for the family as the most important societal structure to transform children into responsible citizens.

The *It* comprised the mission of our family—to raise our sons in an environment that fostered physical, mental, emotional, and spiritual growth, such that they could become mature, independent, and accomplished adults. Absent a family's commitment to a meaningful mission, it's no wonder that children are adrift. Again, this has no required structure for the family—traditional or otherwise. It does require mature adults who make the mission of their family their number one priority.

When a family is clear about its mission, it changes the calculus of daily activities. Clarity about our values as a family defines the family's *It*. A colleague one time gave me a great answer when one of my children wanted to see an age-inappropriate movie at a sleepover with some friends. "In our family, we don't [fill in the blank]." The meta-message is: "Our family's mission (our *It*) is to bring up children who are healthy and well-adjusted without the baggage of seeing movies that may teach beliefs about life, honesty, sex, violence, and so on before they possess the judgment and emotional maturity to sift out what is true and ethical and what is not." The great strength of the phrase, "In *our* family," was that it provided us with a compelling reason for a personal boundary for *our* family without condemning choices his friends' families might make.

Families, teams, clubs, and so on also make it possible for children to experience the power of the *It*—a quest or mission. It's one thing to read about the quest of famous leaders in pursuit of some noble quest, but there's no substitute for experiencing the pursuit of some important goal personally. A coach must inspire the team with a mission. Winning the regional championship or even winning the state championship becomes the mission or purpose for inspired play.

In addition to sports teams, there are now many other great opportunities like robotics clubs or environmental causes that give youth a chance to pursue a meaningful *It*. We need a meaningful *It* in our lives to have a sense of purpose. Have we ever seen a child with a compelling *It* in his or her life who was adrift? An *It* provides the focus and accountability so desperately needed by children today.

The Conundrum of Hardship and Adversity

Watching a child struggle may be one of life's most painful experiences. Helicopter parenting became infamous in recent years—the overly protective parent who immerses themselves in every aspect of their child's life to ensure good outcomes. One of the consequences of a parent's attempts to shield their child from all adversity is that the child misses an opportunity to grow and become resilient through adversity.

When our sons were elementary school age, a favorite tradition for the weekend following Thanksgiving was to travel from Atlanta south to Callaway Gardens, a beautiful environmental preserve in middle Georgia. The weather was usually still mild, and the bike trails seemed endless. Over the several days, we always biked to the hot spots like Mr. Sibley's garden. By far, our favorite stop was the butterfly atrium, reportedly the largest living butterfly exhibit in North America. On sunny days, a thousand butterflies fluttered around the glass facility that had the temperature and humidity of a rain forest.

One afternoon, we listened to one of the guides explaining the various stages of a butterfly's life. In the hours before a butterfly flaps its wings, it must free itself from the hardened chrysalis the insect spun around itself. As the guide talked, we watched several butterflies struggle to get out of their own chrysalis. One butterfly was almost free, held fast by a small piece of the hardened shell. One of the boys asked the guide to just snip the remaining bond so we could see the butterfly take his first flight. Her response was that prematurely helping the butterfly out of the chrysalis dooms it to a life of crawling around the ground. Pushing against the barrier strengthened its wings so it can fly. If getting out was too easy, the wings would not develop the strength to lift the butterfly into the sky and create the unique beauty that we all enjoy.

Anne and I wrestled with when to step in and when to let our sons learn to push back against the barriers in their lives. We knew that muscles get stronger not by ease, but rather by pushing against resistance. Candidly, I struggle with when to intervene if a child is bullied. When a child has the confidence to confront a bully or to fight back, it's good to allow that child to handle it. When a child is suffering on-going emotional or physical harm from a bully or has no way to fight back, such as in cyber-bullying, a parent must insert adult influence. Wisdom is knowing the difference.

I observed in my older son the tremendous benefits of overcoming adversity in one circumstance. The positive outcome beautifully generalized to other areas of his life. An outdoor expedition group invited Jim (who had just turned eight) and me to a wilderness camping experience for a week with other dads and their sons. The wilderness school taught us about stewardship of the environment along with many other outdoor skills, such as repelling and rock climbing, and cooking. Personal hygiene skills were not taught or utilized—we were mountain men who didn't need to shower. These rocks on which we practiced our rock climbing skills were real, and not the manufactured type in sports equipment stores.

One morning we arose to the crisp mountain air at our 8,000-foot elevation campground. After breakfast, our assignment was to use our newly acquired rock climbing skills on a 100-foot vertical rock wall a mile away from our campground. When Jim's turn to scale the wall came, the instructor tied a safety rope around his waist and assured Jim that no matter what, he would not fall to the ground. I understood the concept intellectually until I later clung to small crevices 70 feet above the ground and felt a wave or two of panic, that my belay rope might not work.

Jim climbed about 30 feet up, couldn't figure out how to go up or down, and then panicked. His panic quickly turned to being immobilized on the wall. He began to cry and begged for someone to take him down from the wall. The instructors tried to calm him and give him some encouragement to keep moving, but he could not compose himself. After about 15 minutes, the lead instructor came over and asked me what they should do. It was one of the hardest decisions I've ever made, but I finally said, "Leave him up there." Intuitively, I had a sense that this was a major developmental milestone in his young life that offered great potential for good. Although it may not have given Jim much comfort at the moment, I also knew that the belay rope would prevent any serious injury if he lost his foothold.

Eventually, an instructor climbed within about 10 feet of where Jim clung to the side of the rock wall, still crying. The instructor calmly urged him to study his surroundings. "There's a small ledge about two feet above your head to the left." Jim stopped crying long enough to look at the ledge. In rock climbing, I learned that a move can be the most gut-wrenching part of climbing. You turn loose of everything that feels safe and comfortable to make it to the next point of stability. The instructor quietly encouraged him to reach for the ledge. After what seemed like an eternity, Jim made his move. All the instructors erupted in, "Way to go, Jim. Keep going!" Jim made another difficult move but this time less tentatively. Another and another, always with a chorus of affirmation. Twenty minutes later, he stood atop the wall beaming. Jim repelled down the wall, ran to the instructor, and asked to climb the wall again!

The benefits and power of affirmation may be at a lifetime high when children are in their teens.

Of course, we cannot know what happens inside another person, but by all appearances, Jim turned a major corner in his life that morning. He seemed more confident and more independent and more resilient. Over time, other changes followed—maturity, success in sports, and completion of his Eagle Scout Award.

Adversity is a primary means to develop resilience, so to insulate a child from age-appropriate adversity denies him or her the opportunity to develop this critical quality. My view on the benefits of a child's successfully overcoming adversity is that when paired with affirmation, it can be wonderfully life changing for a growing child. A first-century writer detailed the following four-part sequence that can result from well-handled adversity:

1. Problems and trials
2. Develop endurance
3. Strength of character
4. Confident hope[4]

Wise parents, teachers, and coaches measure the potential benefits of letting a child struggle within a supportive environment to encourage the child to stay the course. Great teachers have a gift of staying just ahead of their students' developmental needs.

Final Counsel to Parents, Teachers, and Coaches

The benefits and power of affirmation may be at a lifetime high when children are in their teens. Words of Life are critical to us no matter what our age, but there is a unique window in a child's life to make their trajectory sound and to bring out the best in them as they make major life decisions about the kind of person he or she will become. To speak Words of Life into a child's core, we must have a sound core ourselves. May all of us who have children or work with children resolve to speak Words of Life into the core of these dear ones!

Notes

1. A. Wolff, "Is the Era of Abusive College Coaches Finally Coming to an End?" *Sports Illustrated*, Sept. 28, 2015, https://www.si.com/college-basketball/2015/09/29/end-abusive-coaches-college-football-basketball.

2. Ibid.

3. Ibid.

4. Romans 5:3–4 (New Living Translation).

12 What Would Happen If We Put This into Practice?

A Call to Action

As a citizen of the United States, I have become somewhat dismayed in recent years about the level of divisiveness and dysfunction in our country. Whether politicians, journalists, celebrities, or just the general populace, *criticism flourishes and affirmation languishes*. How we arrived at this state invites rigorous debate, but the more important question is how do we restore respect, civility, and unity as a country? While I cannot speak with authority, I suspect the same questions plague other nations, as well.

Following 9/11, I was struck by the increase in simple courtesies. Small things like friendlier greetings, holding doors open for others, allowing someone to merge into traffic, and other acts of kindness seemed to rule the day for a few months. We had been humbled as a nation, and it showed. We became nicer people for a while. Against the painful darkness of the assault on our people, there was also a civic kindness not seen in a long while.

Entropy eventually set in, and gradually, we returned to our pre-9/11 preoccupation with our normal lives. Civility seems more difficult for busy people who haven't been humbled recently.

This book asserts that certain actions bring out the best in others, while others bring out the worst. Wouldn't we like to see a lot more bringing out the best in each other? I have expressed many opinions throughout the book, but the major tenants of *Extraordinary Influence* rest upon solid scientific research. For example:

1. Affirmation produces tremendous benefits—physically, emotionally, and socially.

2. Criticism creates tremendous problems—physically, emotionally, and socially.

3. What I labeled *Alliance Feedback* allows us to correct wayward behavior without setting off some of the problems associated with criticism. We connect a person's need to change with important aspirations relevant to the recipient of our feedback.

Most of my workdays are spent in the corporate world. What would happen if we put these principles into practice in the corporate world?

What would happen if we applied these principles more broadly?

My opinion is that:

The research I referenced throughout the book is prescriptive for individuals; however, we as a society would be much more likely to flourish if we became more affirming and less critical. Just imagine that post-9/11 period, except that it's better and it's sustainable.

Think about the amazing world we could create for our organizations, our families, and our communities if affirmation flowed freely and criticism became rare. I keep hearing that we must come together as a country, although to date, I haven't heard anyone say exactly how we're to do that. My answer is, let's just start by making a lot more affirming statements and a lot less diminishing ones.

What if we flipped our normal use of criticism and affirmation—we affirmed people every day and made critical comments a lot less often?

Of course, this notion may require a few clarifications:

- Not all ideas are good—we can evaluate ideas and initiatives and throw out the bad ones. I'm not saying this is *Happy World*, where we do everything someone wants to do at work.

- Despite what I've heard from many people to the contrary, there actually are *dumb questions*. It's okay not to spend resources answering those.

- Not all people are affirmable. Although my grandmother Goldie did like to say, "Nobody's worthless. At least they can be used as a bad example."

With all this in mind, the following is my call to action:

What if we started speaking Words of Life with much greater frequency to members of our family, some of our colleagues at work, and occasionally to a random person we meet?

What if we acknowledge that there is an unlimited supply of affirmation and there is no law that we ration it?

I invite you to join others in voting for a worldwide ban on the phrase, *constructive criticism.* You can do so at www.drtimirwin.com

Please also join the discussion on my website about how we can affirm more and criticize less.

ACKNOWLEDGMENTS

Thank you to my dear wife, Anne, who affirmed and encouraged me throughout this project. My agent, Jan Miller, CEO of Dupree Miller, was a tremendous help in identifying the right publisher for this book and for representing me with great skill and passion. Special thanks to Elizabeth Weaver and Hillary Hope Doyle for their outstanding work in researching and applying the neuropsychology literature supporting the ideas set forth in this book. Richard Narramore, senior editor of Wiley, exercised great insight into how to bring forward the critical themes of the book. It's been a great privilege to work with him. Pete Gaughan and Danielle Serpica who have both been terrific colleagues in bringing this book to life and managing the myriad of details. Caroline Maria Vincent, production editor at Wiley, has been great to work with and efficiently managed the book through production. Peter Knox from the marketing arm of Wiley has shown great support for this book, and I am grateful for his insight and determined sponsorship. Thank you to my Executive Assistant, Lesley Sifford, who pursues excellence in every aspect of her work.

ABOUT THE AUTHOR

Dr. Tim Irwin has consulted with a number of America's most well-known and respected companies. For over 25 years, Dr. Irwin has assisted corporations in diverse industries including fiber optics, real estate, financial services, baby products, information technologies, news and entertainment, insurance, hotels, high-technology research, chemicals, sports marketing, auto parts, military and commercial optics, floor covering, bottling, quick service restaurants, fibers and textiles, electronics, cosmetics, retail clothing, and pharmaceuticals.

Dr. Irwin worked from 2000 to 2005 in senior management of an international consulting firm with over 300 offices worldwide and, following a merger, served on the management team of a *Fortune 500* company. His work has taken him to over 20 foreign countries in Europe, Latin American, Canada, and the Far East.

Prior to *Extraordinary Influence, Dr. Irwin* authored three critically-acclaimed books, including *Impact: Great Leadership Changes Everything*, a *New York Times* bestseller. His earlier books include *Run with the Bulls without Getting Trampled* and *Derailed: Five Lessons Learned from Catastrophic Failures of Leadership*.

Dr. Irwin has contributed to numerous national media outlets including Fox Business News, Fox News Channel, CNBC, *Investor's Business Daily*, *Business Week*, and *The Wall Street Journal*.

Dr. Irwin completed two Ph.D. programs in organizational psychology and clinical psychology and is a frequent speaker on leadership and leadership development. His leadership philosophy maintains that while the actions of a leader are seminal, the core of a leader (what's inside) ultimately determines his or her legacy.

To contact Tim about speaking to your group, please go to: www.drtimirwin.com.

INDEX